MW00450270

SIDESHOW

SIDESHOW

LIVING WITH LOSS AND

MOVING FORWARD WITH FAITH

RICKEY SMILEY

W PUBLISHING GROUP

AN IMPRINT OF THOMAS NELSON

Sideshow

Copyright © 2024 Rickey Smiley

All rights reserved. No portion of this book may be reproduced, stored in a retrieval system, or transmitted in any form or by any means—electronic, mechanical, photocopy, recording, scanning, or other—except for brief quotations in critical reviews or articles, without the prior written permission of the publisher.

Published in Nashville, Tennessee, by W Publishing, an imprint of Thomas Nelson.

Thomas Nelson titles may be purchased in bulk for educational, business, fundraising, or sales promotional use. For information, please email SpecialMarkets@ThomasNelson.com.

Unless otherwise noted, Scripture quotations are taken from the ESV® Bible (The Holy Bible, English Standard Version®). Copyright © 2001 by Crossway, a publishing ministry of Good News Publishers. Used by permission. All rights reserved.

Scripture quotations marked AMP are taken from the Amplified® Bible (AMP). Copyright © 2015 by The Lockman Foundation. Used by permission. www.lockman.org.

Scripture quotations marked NIV are taken from The Holy Bible, New International Version®, NIV®. Copyright © 1973, 1978, 1984, 2011 by Biblica, Inc.® Used by permission of Zondervan. All rights reserved worldwide. www.Zondervan.com. The "NIV" and "New International Version" are trademarks registered in the United States Patent and Trademark Office by Biblica, Inc.®

Scripture quotations marked NLT are taken from the Holy Bible, New Living Translation. © 1996, 2004, 2015 by Tyndale House Foundation. Used by permission of Tyndale House Publishers, Inc., Carol Stream, Illinois 60188. All rights reserved.

Any internet addresses, phone numbers, or company or product information printed in this book are offered as a resource and are not intended in any way to be or to imply an endorsement by Thomas Nelson, nor does Thomas Nelson vouch for the existence, content, or services of these sites, phone numbers, companies, or products beyond the life of this book.

ISBN 978-1-4003-4299-0 (HC)
ISBN 978-1-4003-4303-4 (audiobook)
ISBN 978-1-4003-4302-7 (ePub)
ISBN 978-1-4003-4301-0 (TP)

Library of Congress Control Number: 2024937427

Printed in the United States of America
24 25 26 27 28 LBC 5 4 3 2 1

*To every mother and father who has lost a
child, I love you with all of my heart.
I respect you.
I'm praying for you.*

CONTENTS

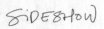
SIDESHOW

PART 3: I AM HEALING

AUTHOR'S NOTE

THIS BOOK WAS HARD TO WRITE, BUT I FELT A CALLING to do so. As I wrote, what poured out was more of a conversation, more of a testimony, than just writing prose. I see this book as a conversation with my own grief, with God, and with you, my reader. The writing style is meant to reflect that. It's meant for you to hear my voice and feel me with you in your own journey. Please consider this book and its writing style as more of a conversation than a memoir.

Rickey

INTRODUCTION

That Sunday

No one ever told me that grief felt so much like fear.
—C. S. Lewis

SHE'D *JUST* TALKED TO HIM THAT MORNING.

"Have you heard from Brandon?" I asked my mother.

She'd been trying to schedule a sit-down between me and my son for a while. We were estranged, and I hadn't seen him in two years. His lifestyle, and the anguish his addiction caused me and his siblings, required me to put some distance between us. But I always thought we'd eventually figure it out—come to some kind of understanding.

"Yeah, I talked to him. He's going to church with me this morning," Mama said.

This was comforting. Brandon's recovery had been a long and winding road for him. For everyone. We'd finally planned a meeting that upcoming week to maybe—hopefully—patch some things up. Again, come to an understanding. I truly believed his recent baptism

SIDESHOW

was a sign that he wanted something different—something more for his life than the ups and downs drugs provided. And that's what I wanted for him. More than he probably knew. More than even I knew.

But on Sunday, January 29, 2023, as I stood in the living room of my Dallas condo, just ten minutes after hanging up with my mother, I got the worst phone call of my life.

"Brandon has OD'd," his girlfriend said between her sobs. "They just rushed him to the hospital."

I said the only thing I knew to say, what I always say: "Everything's going to be all right. Calm down. He'll be fine."

Then I went into dad mode.

I called my mom back and told her to get to the University of Alabama hospital as soon as possible.

Called my daughter and told her to go there too.

Called my assistant and asked her to get me on the next flight to Birmingham, my hometown.

Fielded another call from Brandon's sister as I started packing to leave.

"Yes, I know about it. Everything's going to be fine."

I really thought it would be. I don't know why I thought that. Maybe it was mostly hope.

And then, as I stood in the same spot I had been standing earlier, my phone rang. It was Brandon's sister again and her mother, my ex. They were sobbing.

"Tell me what's happening!" I said.

More crying. Then, those words:

"Brandon died."

I'm pretty sure my heart stopped beating, if only for a second or two.

I'd seen and felt a lot of things in my life, but I had never felt the kind of sickness in my stomach that I did that day.

The room started to spin. I thought I was going to faint.

I have to pull it together.

For them.

For everyone.

So I did not faint. I turned back to dad mode.

I called my mother back. "Where are you?" I asked.

"I'm at the hospital. Outside."

"Okay, listen. He didn't make it. I'm on my way home. Taking the first flight I can get out of DFW."

Tears.

Then I called my son Malik, who was a senior at Alabama State University in Montgomery.

"Hey, listen to me carefully. I need you to get in your truck and go straight home right now, okay? We have an emergency. Brandon OD'd and he didn't make it. Go straight home, do you understand?"

Silence. Then, "Yes, sir."

Then I called both my daughters—Aaryn, who was in Waco, and D'essence, who was already at the hospital. "Hey, try to be careful going into the hospital," I told D'essence. "Go to the emergency room where Mama is, but I need you to know that Brandon didn't make it."

Tears and more tears.

Then—because I am Rickey Smiley, stand-up comedian and host of the *Rickey Smiley Morning Show*, and because I didn't want anyone putting a word out before our family did—I recorded a video for social media:

"Thank you all for your prayers. I wanted to let everybody

know, make an announcement, that my son Brandon Smiley has passed away. Pray for us. Pray for my family."

Then I grabbed my backpack and prepared to leave. Before I could get to the door, though, I heard it. It was loud and clear. As if I were wearing headphones, the words and melody of Jonathan McReynolds's song "God Is Good" played in my head. One line stood out among the rest: "And may your bad days prove that God is good."[1]

That was my hope. And I guess I could have cried right then. I know many people would have, and that's fine. But I didn't have the luxury of tears quite yet. There was no breaking down for me. I had a job to do. I needed to make sure that everyone else was okay. Because that's who I am, and that's what I do.

So I grabbed my keys and shades, locked my door, and got ready to march down the hall to the elevator. But, man oh man, that hallway looked like it could go on forever. As much as I knew I had to get to my family in Birmingham, in that moment, I had no idea how I was going to make it if I couldn't even walk down the hall. The walls along the narrow corridor felt like they were caving in on me, and the designs on the carpet made the walkway look like it was spinning. I knew I had a long way to go. I knew I couldn't let this stop me. So I asked God for help.

"Father, if I can just make it to the elevator, I know I'll be fine."

I made it to the elevator.

When I got to the car that was going to take me to the airport, the driver, realizing who I was, got excited and started talking.

Oh, Lord. Help me.

"Not right now. I can't talk right now," I said to the man. "I need to think. I just suffered a loss." He simply nodded and honored my request.

By the time I arrived at the airport, I had started to receive calls. Ricky Lewis, the national president of my fraternity, Omega Psi Phi Fraternity Incorporated, was one of the first calls I actually answered. Ironically, he was reaching out to discuss Tyre Nichols, the young, unarmed Black man who had been beaten and murdered by police officers in Memphis only a week before. My fraternity brothers were trying to organize a way to help the Nichols family, and I was all in. As he spoke with such passion, I listened intently to what he was saying. I wanted to do my part. I would do my part. But before he got off the phone, I shared the news with him.

"I just wanted you to know that my son just passed. I'm on my way to Birmingham."

He was completely shocked and offered his condolences.

That call was an anomaly, though. I really didn't feel up to talking to people, so I didn't answer calls. At the airport, I started getting text messages from family and close friends. Messages that began with "I'm so sorry" and ended with "Let me know what you need." I was grateful for them, but all I was trying to do was figure out how to keep putting one foot in front of the other. I had to keep moving because, if I'm honest, all I could think about was jumping as high as I possibly could and landing on my neck so I could I die. I was that heartbroken. I was a father who'd suddenly lost his oldest child, and everything was confusing. Nothing made sense. I couldn't find my plane ticket, and even after I did, I couldn't find the gate. I couldn't cry. I couldn't release any emotions yet, so I was quite literally walking around in a daze. Finally, in a brief moment of clarity, I found a Dallas police officer and asked for help.

"Hey, listen, my son just died. Please help me. I'm so confused. I can't think straight. If I could get you to get me to the gate, that would be great."

Thankfully, the police officer did exactly that. He got me through TSA and walked with me to my gate.

And of course, I was still Rickey Smiley, walking through the airport, so people were speaking to me and trying to get my attention.

"Heeeey, Rickey!" a woman said.

"Can I take a picture?" one man asked.

I was nice about it, but I let him know I couldn't. "I just can't right now," I said.

They didn't know. All they knew was that they'd just seen Rickey Smiley walking through the airport. And because they couldn't have known what was going on, there was no need for me to be rude. I whispered more in the man's ear: "Listen, my son just passed. I'm trying to get home. My mind ain't right."

He immediately understood and didn't take it personally. In fact, the man hugged me, and his girlfriend came over and hugged me too. "We're going to pray for you, man," he said.

Angels.

When we arrived at the gate, there was no line, and the flight was just about to close. The gate agent, however, held the door open for me, and as I got closer, I saw the recognition in her eyes.

"Oh my God, Rickey Smiley," she said. "I've got to get a picture."

Again, people didn't know. They were just happy to see me. And

I'm always thankful for that. But I just couldn't smile and take a picture with her.

I turned to her and said, "Listen, I can't. My mind is not right in this moment. I just found out my son passed, and I have to fly home."

Y'all, I saw her face turn in real time. She went from being an excited fan to a prayer warrior in half a second. This woman I'd never met before ushered me across the threshold and shut the door. She then walked me halfway down the Jetway before stopping and grabbing both my hands, squeezing them tight. Then she prayed. I mean, that sister held the whole flight up and prayed for me so good that afterward I knew I'd get home with no problem. Then she looked at me and said, "I'm your fellow church member, Rickey." Come to find out, she attended the same church I did in Dallas, Friendship-West Baptist Church.

As I said, I had no idea who that lady was. If she walked up to me today, I would have a hard time recognizing her because that's how messed up I was that day. All I remember is that when the angel of a police officer dropped me off at the gate, she picked up where he left off.

Another angel.

And God wasn't done. When I got on the plane, the first seat was available. Now, if you've ever flown Southwest Airlines, you know good and well that if you are the last one to walk on a sold-out flight, it's highly likely you are going to be seated in the back where the chairs don't recline and the scent of a not-so-fresh bathroom will be with you the entire time. Thank God that wasn't my portion that day.

It really did seem like God was positioning people every step of the way to ensure that, in my mental and emotional state, I got home to my people. And that included while I was in that first seat on the plane.

When I sat down, I finally tried to take it all in. I kept reminding myself of the song that had shown up in my brain and heart hours earlier. *May my bad days prove that God is still good.*

That's when someone tapped me on the shoulder. He was a Black man, maybe in his late sixties or early seventies (you can't tell with us sometimes).

"Hey, Rickey Smiley! I listen to your show every morning," he said.

I turned halfway around, shook his hand, and said, "Thank you."

Then we took off. As soon as we were in the air, that plane started jerking and bouncing all around the sky. The weather was real bad, cloudy and windy. But I wasn't afraid of the turbulence. I saw everyone around me getting quiet and nervous as the plane dropped, twisted, and turned, but I was just fine. In fact, I could not care less what happened. At that point, if the plane had crashed, I wouldn't have cared a single bit. Nothing mattered.

When we finally reached an altitude where the weather smoothed out, the man behind me tapped me on the shoulder again. This time, he was showing me his phone.

"Man, I just went to a family reunion," he said. "Ain't seen my brothers and sisters for years." I took his phone and scrolled through the photos. The images were nice. Family laughing and smiling. I listened as he shared all the fun he had, all the shenanigans that happened at the reunion. His excitement was infectious. The light in his eyes as he walked me through each picture held me captive in a good way. We talked the entire flight.

I never told the man what I was going through. I didn't share with him that my son had died. I just received his kindness. He kept my mind occupied.

Angel.

When the wheels of the plane finally hit the tarmac at Birmingham-Shuttlesworth International, I turned my phone back on. Whatever brief rest that conversation in the sky gave me was over. Reality hit me again. Brandon was still gone. And I easily had over two hundred text messages reminding me of that. The video I'd posted before I left had gone viral.

"Hey, Rickey, I'm sorry for your loss."

"Brother, let me know what you need. I'm here."

"Oh man, I can't believe it. My condolences."

I couldn't respond to anyone.

When I walked off the plane, it was clear that the tone had shifted on the ground too. Whereas the news hadn't made it to the people I met at the Dallas airport, it had certainly reached folks in Birmingham.

"Hey, Rickey, man, I'm so sorry," I heard from many people as I moved through the terminal.

If there's one thing I know for sure, Birmingham don't play about me. I am a son of the city. They not only know me, they also knew my son. So I could feel the love and support as I made my way through the airport and out to the car where all three of my uncles waited. I'd told them I had no baggage—just a backpack—so they waited for me by the car on the upper level. These are my dad's brothers—Uncle Bruh (Eugene), Uncle Suge (Bandy), and the baby, Uncle Bruce (Anthony). Every last one of them with the last name Smiley. Every last one of them greeted me with tears in their eyes.

When we got in the car, I quickly turned the radio to 98.7 KISS to try to lighten the mood. I did what I always did and let them know that everything would be all right eventually.

"Come on, y'all. We're going to be okay. We're fine. We're going to be fine," I said.

I didn't want them to cry. I mean, I hadn't even cried yet. And I'll share more about why later on. But in that moment, the things that were holding me together were the songs that kept me grounded— like Jonathan McReynolds's—and poems like "Invictus," which I'd learned while pledging Omega Psi Phi.

> Out of the night that covers me,
> Black as the pit from pole to pole,
> I thank whatever gods may be
> For my unconquerable soul.
>
> In the fell clutch of circumstance
> I have not winced nor cried aloud.
> Under the bludgeonings of chance
> My head is bloody, but unbowed.[2]

I was pulling from everything I knew, including the shield of Omega Psi Phi, to get my strength. So it makes sense that those words played over and over again in my head. To make it through that day and the days to come, I had to view this tragedy like just another pledge process where I needed to learn the lessons so I could cross whatever lay ahead for me and my family.

I was mostly quiet in the car for the remainder of the ride to my Birmingham house. As soon as we pulled up, I saw Miss Pat standing in the window. She is someone who has been a part of my family for what seems like forever. I not only went to church with her for the longest time, but Miss Pat helped me raise my kids and grandson.

As soon as I walked through the door, I saw her tears. "You okay, Miss Pat? It's going to be okay," I said. Because again, that's who I am. It's my job to make sure everyone is okay.

Since it was Sunday and right smack in the middle of the NFL playoffs, I turned the game on once I got settled and people started to show up. I could feel that everyone's emotions were right on the surface, so I tried to make it so that the atmosphere wasn't as heavy and raw. My neighbor brought over some food. A classmate I texted, Desi, brought over more food. There wasn't a bunch of people there, just close family and friends. I was grateful for the privacy many gave me when I first arrived back in Birmingham because, honestly, I was a mess on the inside and knew I wouldn't remotely feel like myself until I saw my other son, Malik, walk through the door. When he finally did, there was only one thought that crossed my mind: *This is the only son I have left.*

So why am I starting here? Why am I opening this book with the most devastating thing that's ever happened to me in my entire life? Well, because it's the most devastating thing that's ever happened to me in my entire life. The death of my son marks the point when everything changed. When you lose a child, you are not the same. Don't let anybody tell you different. You are inducted into a special club that no one wants to be in. You can't begin to understand anything I write about unless you first know that this terrible thing colors everything I will do going forward and everything I remember about the past. Ultimately, I'm writing this book because I want to share what I've gone through with the hope that somebody reading it will be able to identify with it and begin their own journey toward healing.

The truth is, none of us is getting out of this world alive. If you haven't had any significant losses, the hardest thing I can tell you is: it is coming. Those losses are inevitable. But I believe it's the support of the people around you that helps you survive the grief when it does come.

At the end of every one of my stand-up performances, I go to the edge of the stage to shake hands with the audience. And almost every time, I can recognize the people who have lost children. They have a kind of sadness in their eyes even as they are smiling and laughing with me. It's like walking down a dark alley and encountering zombies. They are moving and seem alive, but their eyes are dark. The light is gone. The only difference for me now is that, when I see them, I'm forced to realize that I am one of them too.

But I keep telling jokes. I keep laughing. Even when it feels like I have caught some awful disease that makes me different than I was before. Because telling jokes is my job. It's my calling. For me, doing comedy is like walking. It's a part of who I am and what I do. And guess what? Just like I can walk and chew gum, I can tell jokes and be sad.

And maybe that's why I named this book *Sideshow*. I'll talk more about my love of music, and the impact of '70s soul music on my life in particular, but when I think about what my life has been like since Brandon died, I'm reminded of the song "Sideshow"— sung by the '70s soul group Blue Magic. When they sing, "There's got to be no sadder show to see," my heart swells with recognition.[3] Because it's true. Losing a child has made my life feel like a circus in many ways. The kind of circus where all the laughter and entertainment is up front, but if someone is even remotely discerning, they'll see the weariness in the eyes of that trapeze artist or the exhaustion on the face of the clown. Because of what I do, I'm called on to perform all the time. I'm called on to laugh and bring joy. But I suspect that if folks were to look really closely, they'd see something else. They'd see the pain of my loss right on the surface, the tears waiting to fall. Like Smokey Robinson and the Miracles sang in their hit song "The Tears of a Clown," "Now if there's a smile on my face, it's only there trying to fool the public."[4]

But I still do it. I still show up on the stage. No matter what. Because I really do believe that laughter is medicine. There have been days when I've literally gone from crying my eyes out in my dressing room to cracking on some man or woman on the front row of my show and having the whole audience nearly passed out with uncontrollable laughter. Then, as if I haven't spent hours with a smile on my face, I'll cry all the way back to my hotel room. There have been times on my radio show when a wave a grief hits me so hard during a commercial that I have literally laid down on the floor next to my desk. But the minute that mic comes back on? *Boom*. I'm turning on my joy.

Cracking these jokes has kept me alive. It was and is a kind of therapy for me. It has kept my mind occupied.

This is my life now.

So if I can drop even just a few nuggets to you about how you can manage your grief—because no, it never goes away—then that's what I want to do in these pages. Consider this book your permission slip to put both your pride and religion aside and go get therapy. That's what I had to do. God created therapists just the same as He created doctors. If your ankle were broken, you'd go to the doctor, so why wouldn't you go when your mind is hurting?

I know there are people listening to the *Rickey Smiley Morning Show* who have also lost their children. They are counting on my jokes to get them through their day. I had my son for thirty-two years, but there's someone out there who had hers for only seventeen. That's motivation enough for me. If I don't keep going for me, I'm going to try to keep going for them. And it's not just about those who are grieving the loss of a child. I also tell jokes for the person on their way to dialysis. For that person who is getting chemotherapy. If anything, Brandon's death has taught me that it's not about me. It *can't* be all about me. I must continue to keep going so I can heal, yes, but also so that I fulfill my purpose.

In short, I've got an axe to grind.

More than ever, I feel like I must go out into the world and make *it* happen. Success. More joy. Helping others. I feel compelled to do it not just for me but for Brandon. My son was a performer as well. He was following in my footsteps and becoming a professional comedian. And now that he's gone, when I'm onstage, I find that I'm doing it for me *and* him. It's personal.

For the longest time, I used to say I only wanted to make my grandparents proud. I believe I did that. They were overjoyed when they saw me on BET's *Comic View* every night. I knew exactly what it meant to see their grandbaby doing all that I was doing, especially since their son, my father, died of his own addiction before seeing his dreams come true. But now, my grandparents have long been in glory, and I'm doing this for Brandon.

I'm funnier now than I've ever been, all because of that axe. My purpose has shifted. I walk onstage with a whole different approach. I know my boy doesn't want me sitting around stressed, depressed, and worried. In so many ways, he's let me know that he's in a better place, that he's not suffering anymore. And because I know he is at peace, I can be also.

Here's to making you proud, son. Let the sideshow begin.

PART ONE

I AM A SON

*Honor your father and your mother, that
your days may be long in the land that
the* Lord *your God is giving you.*

Exodus 20:12

1

HOLDING BACK THE TEARS

Love recognizes no barriers. It jumps
hurdles, leaps fences, penetrates walls to
arrive at its destination full of hope.

–Maya Angelou

IT TOOK ME A WHILE TO CONNECT THE DOTS, BUT there is a reason I couldn't immediately cry when I learned my son had passed. A reason that takes this story, my story, all the way back to April 11, 1974, and the saddest day of my life up until Brandon's death. All the way back to my own father's funeral.

I was six years old when my dad died. And as it sometimes happens, I got a bit lost in all the preparations and grieving my family did right after learning the news. Things had to get done. Most Black folks, especially the ones who grow up in the South like I did, ask the same questions when someone dies: "Who's doing the

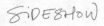

body? Can Lil' Man or Big Boy be one of the pallbearers? Where is the repast?" And adjacent to that, "Who's cooking?" So that's what my family was taking care of. They'd busied themselves with flowers and flags (my father fought in Vietnam), obituaries and suit selection. And in the meantime, there was a little boy watching it all who was grieving a father he didn't know as well as he'd have liked.

For the most part, I was a very happy-go-lucky kid. I liked to have fun. To laugh. Clearly, that hasn't changed much. But more than anything, I found so much comfort in being around my grandparents on both sides. They all practically raised me. For several reasons, including the loss of my dad and my mother's own struggle with addiction during my teen years, my grandparents became more like my parents, and my great-grandparents were more like grandparents. I was their son, and because of them, I had a foundation that was so doggone solid, it's unbelievable to think about at times.

The story of my grandparents is such an interesting one. As God would have it, both sets of my grandparents ended up being neighbors on the same street in Birmingham. On my father's side, my granddaddy and grandma crossed paths at Parker High School, with their love story kicking off soon after Granddaddy graduated. On my mother's side, my grandma, though raised in Birmingham, was originally from Columbus, Georgia, where she was only able to complete a fifth-grade education but still drove home the importance of me "getting my schooling." I had a family who didn't just get together every now and again but who stuck with each other through some wild things and did the best they could. In doing so, they built a community where children—cousins, friends, and godchildren—floated in and out of homes knowing there were adults who believed that love meant taking care of one another.

My grandparents were truly the heart and soul of my life growing up and gave me the best of everything they had. They weren't rich. Not materially, anyway. My grandmother worked at the airport, and my granddad worked many different jobs throughout his life. They had a brick home in a nice neighborhood, but there still weren't a lot of extras. Whatever they might have lacked financially, though, they were filthy rich in love and compassion. And they spared no expense when it came to loving me.

In hindsight, I realize the greatest gift my grandparents ever gave me was their presence. They were always available. Whether I found myself going to Grandmom's (on my mother's side) house or my dad's parents' house, there was never a time when there wasn't a clean room, good food, and lots of love available. They also provided much of the discipline and structure a Black boy growing up in Alabama in the 1970s and '80s needed.

This isn't to say that my mom wasn't there. She was always a physical presence, even if there were times in the latter part of my childhood when she couldn't be an emotional one. When my sister and I were really young, our relationship with our mother was so strong. I will always credit her for giving me something that would define the rest of my life: music and the stage. I am a musically driven comedian and performer because of her.

Mama loved music. I mean, she *loved* loved it. And from the time I could walk, she took me to nearly every one of her favorite concerts. I'll never forget the time I went to see James Brown in concert. I couldn't have been more than seven years old. They had this best-dressed contest going on, and there I was standing next to this other little boy sitting on my row, both of us dressed like little men. I had on a white suit, a light blue shirt, and a white bow tie—the same thing I had worn to my dad's funeral less than a year before. My hair was styled in the cleanest Afro blowout. When they called all the contestants up to the stage, the crowd went wild when they saw these two mannish little boys. You know Black folks love to see a "baby" dressed to impress!

"Oooh, baby boy, look at you! You sharp as a tack."

"You clean, lil' man! Cleaner than the board of health."

I could hear all the praise from the stage, and it made my heart grow so big in my little chest. There were a lot of grown people primping and posing on that stage too. They all looked good in their bell-bottom suits, Afros, and hats. But when they let the audience of five thousand people in Boutwell Auditorium decide the winner of the contest, the response was overwhelmingly in favor of me and the other little boy. Faces greasy and smiling wide, we both won a hundred dollars and were taken backstage to meet Ben E. King from the Drifters, who opened the show with his hit song "Supernatural Thing," and, of course, the Godfather of Soul himself, James Brown.

You *must* understand what it meant for a little Black boy like me to meet one of the most prolific Black artists of the day. A man who sang "Say It Loud—I'm Black and I'm Proud"[1] and made us believe that was true. James Brown was a Black man like me who came from the South—born in South Carolina and raised in Augusta, Georgia—and who "got it out the mud" as these young folks like to say nowadays. I was in awe.

The award money was also a huge unexpected blessing for us as a family. Mama took it and bought much-needed dressers for me and my sister, plus a big yellow Tonka truck for me. I played and played with that truck so much that year. It was a prize I treasured.

No matter what was going on—death and the grief that followed—our family knew how to keep on living. I was going to get all the things I needed from the various people who could provide them. Mama made sure I had music and art and passion in my life, and my grandparents made sure I had the foundation of faith and discipline.

My dad? Well, that's a more complicated story.

When people ask me about my relationship with my dad to try to figure out what shaped me, it sounds harsh to say that his death impacted me more than anything he ever did in his life. But that's the truth. That's not to say I didn't love him, because I did, in the way all little boys love their fathers. It's more because I didn't *know* him. Dad left for Vietnam shortly after I was born, and that experience changed him and the trajectory of our relationship forever. He saw some horrifying stuff over there—friends getting killed, dropping napalm, all the things you read about or watch in the movies. My uncle Herbert, my mom's brother who left for Nam with my dad, once shared with me just how hard and gruesome the experience was, and I never forgot the images he painted.

Vietnam was also where Dad's struggle with drugs started. I guess it made what he and other soldiers were seeing easier to deal with—easier to survive. Then, add to the trauma of war having to return to the US and still be confronted with what it meant to be a Black man from the South in *this* country and, yeah, I absolutely understand how he could never be the same.

The thing is, everyone in my life had an image of my father from before the war except me. He was a man they loved deeply. A man who moved with a kind of freedom and swag that drew people to him. But that is not who he was when he returned, so that's not who I knew. After the war, he came back to Birmingham briefly before moving to New York. I'm not sure if it was the bad memories or the ghosts he thought would always chase him down, the ones he tried to extinguish with drugs and alcohol, but Dad rarely returned home to the South. The memories of him that I can recall, the ones that loom large for me, are the times when I talked to him on the phone, long distance.

The very last time I spoke to my father, I was sitting in the hallway of my grandmother's house. I'd pulled the long cord of the phone there so I could listen and savor every word he said. My grandma was on the other end of the line, in the kitchen, so Dad could talk to us both at the same time.

"I know you're going to look out for him," Dad said to her.

"Yeah, you know I will. Don't you worry about Rickey, now. He'll be just fine."

A few weeks later, my father was dead.

What does it mean to know your father but not have his presence? If I'm honest, I'm not sure. I know for some people it's absolutely devastating. The absence of a father can send them to a dark place. It can ultimately lead to emotional trauma and sometimes manifest in various forms of acting out or coping mechanisms. For many, having a father who is not just physically present but also emotionally and spiritually supportive is important to their development. Growing up without the guidance of a father leaves a mark, causing them to feel abandoned. Ironically though, I can't say the lack of my father's presence was all that detrimental for me.

I'm sure this might surprise some, given the common and often false narrative surrounding absent fathers, particularly in the Black community. But I attribute my resilience to the role played by my village. In fact, the biggest factor for me being okay is that I *did* have the presence of my grandfather and uncles—all who served as father figures and representatives of what a man should be in my life. My grandfather and uncles didn't just fill the void left by my father; they actively participated in my upbringing, imparting wisdom and shaping my understanding of masculinity and responsibility. They took me on adventures, showed me things, and shared their knowledge about the world. For better or worse, they taught me about women. They taught me how to move through the world and instilled in me values that continue to guide my actions and decisions. Their presence meant I didn't necessarily feel many negative effects of my father's absence. My family stood in the gap for me. There could have been lack. There could have been feelings of abandonment. There could have been lots of pain. But instead, there was love. There was discipline. There was guidance. And I'm grateful for it all.

It's so important that we do that for our family members, for the people we love. Standing in the gap, being present and willing to meet a need when there is one—that's what community does. It also teaches us to show compassion and empathy for all people— whether they are close to us or not—who may not have the same circumstances as we do. I'm certain that one of our greatest callings is to be the ones who stand in the gap for those who are suffering. For those who have experienced loss. For those in pain.

That said, I realize my own desire to be present in my children's lives may have been influenced by what I experienced with my father. I don't think anyone can deny that I'm an engaged father. When I can (and, clearly, when the relationship has not become too toxic to continue), I always want to be a source of guidance, support, and unwavering love. I'm not interested in my children just *knowing* me. That's not good enough. I want to be present in their lives. I don't want to just have the occasional phone call or just be the one who buys them things. I want to be part of their lives if I can. I want to have open communication with them and create a safe space for vulnerability. That is true from my oldest to my youngest.

I do think that some of the reasons why Brandon and I bumped heads so much has everything to do with me wanting to be present in his life. I *wanted* to know what was going on with him. I asked him questions. I took him everywhere. I exposed him to a way of life that was successful—my professional and financial wins were, in a way, his too—and different from what some of his friends might have known growing up in Atlanta (where he spent the first half of his childhood with his mom and stepdad) and Alabama (where he spent the latter half when he came to live with me). I let him know and see and experience things so he would understand what kind of wonderful life was possible for him—if he lived right.

So now, I guess in the same way I wonder about what it means to know your father but not have his presence, I also wonder if it's possible to be present for and yet still not know your child—at least in the ways that you long to know them. Because I think despite all the things I tried to do for him—fighting for more time in drawn-out custody battles with his mother, wanting him to be with me, sharing with him, talking to him, asking him questions—there was still a part of himself he held back. A part of himself he couldn't share with me.

Maybe it was because he knew I stood on the side of the up-and-up, the straight and narrow. I never believed a person had to drink and smoke and do whatever the in crowd was doing to fit in and be successful. But that, in part, was the life he wanted to live. Sure, there is a part of me that certainly gets it. I was young once. I wanted to party with my friends and hang out. But there was something in me that drew the line, not just for myself but later for my children. I think once Brandon saw the line I'd drawn, he just wasn't willing or able—once addiction set in—to cross over to my side in order to increase the connection between us.

Even now as I think about that, it's a hard thing to accept. I've had to grapple with my feelings of frustration and disappointment. I've certainly questioned whether there was more I could have done to bridge the gap between us. This healing process involves accepting

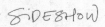

the limitations of my role as a father. While I can provide guidance and support, I couldn't force my son to conform to my expectations or beliefs. His journey was his own, shaped by his experiences, values, and aspirations. As much as I desired a deeper connection with him, I had to acknowledge and accept that he was going to make whatever choices he needed to as the adult he was. He was grown.

Yes, you always have your regrets in life, but there is also a part of you that must accept that you did all you could with what you knew, and that's enough. You do your best and pray God does the rest. In our case, the healing Brandon needed and wanted just happened to be available only on the other side of glory.

———————

It's evident to me now just how much sitting in the funeral for my father all those years ago both changed my life and prepared me for what was to come many years later. But maybe not exactly in the way many would think. Yes, I was a little boy who'd lost his father. A father he'd barely gotten to know. A father whose demons from the war and battle with addiction made his life a rocky existence at best. But what changed me the most was watching the people in my life who gave me the most stability, who were truly my rocks, completely break down in a way that scared me. My grandparents lost it at the funeral of their son, and I'd hardly ever even seen them cry before. I watched in a kind of muted terror as I saw each person I loved cave in to their grief. I kept my eyes on my grandfather especially, who was walking back and forth, handling all the business of the ceremony, and making sure everybody else was okay. I remember thinking to myself, *Grandaddy is doing all that walking around, but why isn't he coming to see about me? I know he sees me.*

And knowing me, I probably said something like that, too, because I remember my mama whispering in my ear, "He's just real busy right now." And that was it. Eventually, he did sit down next to my grandmother. And that's when I saw his tears. I was shook after that. It was the first time I felt like my soul left my body as a kid, seeing them suffer that way.

And it wasn't just them. It was nearly every family member around me. All the people who made me feel safe were utterly broken. My grandmother, wearing an orange and white dress with a diagonal black stripe, didn't even come to the funeral home to view the body before the ceremony because she couldn't stand to see her son that way. Uncle Suge—who was sitting on the end of the pew near me, Mama, my grandparents, and my great-grandparents—held his head down with his eyes closed. My aunt Margaret and uncle Jesse sat on the front row, in the middle, and their faces were wet with tears. I watched my uncle Bruh, my dad's younger brother, sitting on the front row in his Marine uniform and sobbing. Again, I know *now* that Uncle Bruh knew a different person than I did. My father, as I'd known him, wasn't the larger-than-life, protective older brother. The one who taught Uncle Bruh all the things he needed to know growing up. There were memories he held in his heart that spilled out in his cries.

My mother, at one point in the service, put her hand over her face and was crying. This was a man she loved. A man she'd grown up with on that same street where their families lived. She was

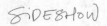

heartbroken. And being a kid, I tried to move her hand from her face, but she wouldn't budge. It seemed to me like she was trying to hide her tears, but I wasn't sure from whom. From me? From the family? From herself? When they called the family up during the service, she took my hand, and we walked toward the blue casket. Then someone—I can't remember who—picked me up so I could see my dad better. He'd grown his hair out and it was greased and combed to the back. They had an American flag over the bottom half of the casket to honor his military service. And then we went back to our seats.

All of this tore me up on the inside. And like I said, it changed me. Even at six years old, I knew right then that if I should ever face such a tremendous loss like they did—especially the loss of a child—I would never let my children and grandchildren see me break down like that. I firmly believe in 1 Timothy 5:8, which says, "If anyone does not provide for his relatives, and especially for members of his household, he has denied the faith and is worse than an unbeliever."

Provision isn't just about food and cars and clothes. Emotional stability is also a way we can provide for our children. And that's what I believed I was doing when, sure enough, I found myself in the exact same position as my grandparents. When Brandon passed away, I chose to keep my sorrow at bay in the beginning. I instinctually knew that seeing that display of wild grief at six years old was too much for me then, and it would be too much for my own children and grandchildren later.

So, like I'd promised myself, I didn't break down. At least not when I first got the news. I had a few moments later that week, but for the most part, I did what my six-year-old eyes watched my granddaddy do. I took care of things. Even on the day of Brandon's funeral, I made sure everyone else was okay. I walked all around that building, tending to the business of laying my boy to rest. And when I got back to my seat, I cried some, I worshipped, but I didn't allow anyone to see me fall apart. I lifted my hands in praise as gospel artist Le'Andria Johnson sang "God Is" by James Cleveland and had practically every person in that Faith Chapel sanctuary on their feet, crying out. I jumped up and down in worship as the preacher delivered the eulogy. But I did not wail. I did not crumble. Not yet. I held it as long as I could.

I could have, though. No one would have blamed me if I did. Maybe there was even a part of me that wished I would have just fallen out right then and there when I got the news. Or do like I've seen some folks at a Black homegoing service and try to practically jump in the casket with their loved ones. But whenever that thought rose in my mind, I looked over at my granddaughter. Brandon's daughter was watching her pop-pop just like I'd watched mine. She knew me as the one she laughed and played with. The one she counted on. When they showed Brandon's pictures on the jumbotron at the church, I heard her say, "Pop-Pop?" because she thought it was me. When I praised God, she would mimic me and lift her little hands in praise. When I shook my head, she did too. There was no doubt that my grandbaby was watching me to see how I would respond to a tragedy she was still too young to comprehend. Periodically, I would go talk to her. Hold her. And that's when I remembered my six-year-old self. How confused and sad and uncertain I was when I saw my grandparents, who I had no doubt loved me, disintegrate into grief the way they did. How I longed for my own granddaddy to stop and acknowledge me. So I sucked up my tears in the beginning. That was the way I knew I could love my grandbaby. I stood ten toes down in my resolve to never make her feel the way I had.

But as you might know, grief is not as obedient as we'd often like it to be. It won't hide, and it's never quiet for long before it demands our surrender. My tears were coming.

2

FAITH AND FUNKADELIC

Life is for the living. Death is for the dead. Let
life be like music. And death a note unsaid.
—LANGSTON HUGHES

I WASN'T LYING WHEN I SAID THAT MUSIC WAS A HUGE part of my childhood. Everybody—and I do mean *everybody*—around me poured music into my life. Plus, growing up in Birmingham meant I was automatically influenced by the convergence of several genres of music: gospel, blues, R&B, country, funk, rock and roll, and later, hip-hop. Still, my mama was my musical guide. She was kind of like the DJ of my early years, spinning records that weren't just random melodies but became the very soundtrack of my whole life. I'm not even sure she realizes it, but she was the one who helped me connect the music to the stage. By

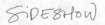

taking me to those concerts as a little kid, she affirmed my desire to perform, and while comedy is where I landed, music is still a thread in anything I do.

The night Marvin Gaye took the stage at Rickwood Field is etched in my memory. Dressed in a white shirt, a black bow tie, and a crushed-velvet green suit, this brother was the epitome of all things Black and smooth. The women in the room were losing their minds. The atmosphere was heated, and the energy was somehow wild and focused at the same time. With dancers moving sensuously in the background, Marvin performed his hits and took us all the way out. The crowd went crazy during songs like "How Sweet It Is" and "Let's Get It On." That was one of many moments when music—Black music in particular—became a part of my DNA.

Funkadelic, too, left their mark on me in those early years. My mama, her friends, and I attended one of their concerts, and the experience was nothing short of electrifying. It was standing room only in the venue, and the lack of seats only contributed to the atmosphere in the room. We were family. This was a community. And yes, there was a grown man on stage wearing a diaper—George Clinton was known for his shenanigans—which blew my young mind, but it still just felt right.

Later, as there became more distance between me and Mama, I found other ways to connect with music. Her older brothers exposed me to artists that were considered "outside the box" where I'm from. They didn't just stick to the Black classics. They threw in Gerry Rafferty, the Eagles, and Steely Dan. To this day, you'll hear "Baker Street" on repeat as I cruise the Gulf or Atlantic Ocean in my boat. During commercial breaks on the *Rickey Smiley Morning Show*, you might find me randomly singing Fleetwood Mac's "Rhiannon" or Elton John's "Tiny Dancer."

My great-grandmother—we called her Big Mama—had a thing for country music. Whenever I was over and even dared trying to switch the radio to gospel, thinking I'd score some points because it was churchy, she'd switch it right on back to the country station, saying, "I've been listening to Hank Williams longer than you've been alive, boy." I mean, what could I really say to that? She was right. And in the end, I fell in love with a little country too. Broadening my musical palate was probably the best thing that could have happened to me, especially considering that the bulk of my career ended up being in radio.

I think, in some ways, I associate most music from the early years of my childhood, the 1970s, with both love and grief. I mean, a Stylistics or Delfonics song can come on and I will feel like I'm right back on that pew with my grandparents mourning my dad. Remember Blue Magic's "Sideshow"? Well, that song actually takes me back to leaving the cemetery with my family. "For the Love of Money" by the O'Jays was the first song I heard in the car after my dad's funeral.

"Some people got to have it . . ."[1]

But what's interesting now is that those same songs also remind me of Brandon. And I know that doesn't make logical sense. Brandon wasn't born in the '70s. He wasn't there with me when I lost my dad. But then again, was he? I don't get too caught up in all

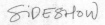

the ancestry, generational talk—not because I don't believe it but because I don't understand a lot of it. But I cannot deny that there is a strong connection in my body when I hear a song from that era. I cannot deny that this connection seems to link backward to my dad and forward to my son. Maybe the grief and pain I saw in my grandparents as a six-year-old was the same grief and pain I desperately felt but couldn't express when I lost Brandon. Again, I know it sounds crazy, but it all makes perfect sense in my world.

Nevertheless, the love of music didn't just come from the soul music I heard as a child. Not even just the R&B, funk, country, and pop music I was exposed to. In fact, if I'm honest, the first rhythms I heard were the handclaps of the choirs at church. The first riffs and runs I fell in love with were of Sister So-and-So who tore down the service every Sunday. Whether it was through music or truth-telling through the preaching, my faith and upbringing in the church primed me for anything and everything I would know and love later.

My grandparents taught me about Jesus. They took me to church, read the Bible to me, and made sure I understood that I would not—*could not*—get very far in life without faith in the One who created me, the One who would carry me through the great, good, bad, and downright ugly of life and living. Because of this, I'm not only a believer but I hold sacred the traditions of the Black church. Yes, I crack jokes about what goes on there. There could be no Bernice Jenkins character without my having been raised in a Black Baptist church in the South. But my comedy ain't never been about mockery or putting down the church. If anything, it highlights the humanity of my people who spend every Sunday in the four walls of somebody's church house, holding on to the hope that their lives, individually and collectively, could be better.

Now, I'm not going to say I was the perfect little church boy. That would be a straight-up lie from the pits of hell, and anybody who attended New Mount Olive Baptist Church would tell you so. I was just your typical little boy, trying my best to do right but falling into mischief every now and again. Especially in Sunday school. Listen, my Sunday school teacher, Sister Hattie Freeman, played no games with Little Rickey. Nevertheless, she was still a guiding presence for me. It was those Sunday school lessons that led me to confess my acceptance of Jesus as my Lord and Savior at seven years old and ultimately get baptized. The absence of a baptismal pool at our church meant we had to go to a sister church for the ceremony. I'll never forget standing in the pool at Groveland Missionary Baptist Church on a Wednesday night, about to get dunked like a human french fry. *Well, this is a whole new level of church experience*, I thought. Maybe it's cliché to say I came up from being submerged in water a different person, but it was true. Even as a kid, I knew the significance of choosing to walk in faith. I was so happy that evening. Even happier when my grandparents and mama treated me to ice cream after the baptism service.

After Sunday school, the whole church would pile into the sanctuary to hear a powerful sermon by Pastor Edward Gardner. Pastor Gardner was one of Dr. King's soldiers in the civil rights movement and a leader in the Southern Christian Leadership Conference (SCLC). He knew how to bring the church down with a word, yes,

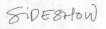

but he also made no bones about the fact that being a part of our church meant not only aligning ourselves with Christ but also with the ongoing fight for justice. Hence why most people in our congregation held active memberships in the SCLC and the NAACP.

Regardless, or maybe *because* of that duality of spiritual food and social responsibility, the church was the place where the light lived for me as a kid. And I mean that in every way. There was the light of church mothers who made sure we were doing right. The light of deacons and pastors who served folks well. The radiant light of the literal sun that would stream through the church window during Sunday school—something I always noticed for some reason. Now, many years away from those days but still attending church on the Sundays my schedule allows, I hold fast to that light, especially as I navigate grief and loss.

One of the challenges of grief is that sometimes the pain of our loss causes us to disconnect from God. In the immediate days and months and maybe even years after our loved one passes on, we still find ourselves not understanding what has happened. We're confused and angry—yes, there's so much anger, especially when we've defined the death of a loved one as senseless or premature. We place the blame on God and tell Him we don't understand how He could be good and still allow these things to happen. Listen, I don't pretend to have all the answers when it comes to that. I have many of those same questions. But here's one thing I do know: the paradox of this journey is that the same God I may question regarding the loss of my son is the same God who is helping me to hold on and survive that loss.

This is why I don't question or judge anyone who struggles

with their faith after a loss. But I do know the presence of God has always been healing for me as I navigate all the stages of my grief. God has become the only one I can turn to, even in my anger. There are times when I express myself in prayer, and I share my anger, frustration, or confusion with Him, with the understanding that as I move through those emotions, there are simply things I'm never going to understand. But that doesn't mean God isn't God. It does mean God is greater than me. I believe He not only allows us to express our feelings to Him but He also provides the immediate support of our family, friends, and those around us. In this way, we can see His loving hand guiding us through the hard times.

Some people also become disconnected from their family and friends or anyone else who might support them through their grief, not realizing that God might be using those people to help. And yes, it's true that not everyone has a support system. That's a reality. For this reason, I understand why people may sometimes turn to the bar or casino or make other unhealthy choices post-loss. Essentially, they are seeking some degree of support to help them get through. Which is even more reason why I encourage people not to disconnect from their faith. Because through prayer, they can actively seek support in whatever shape or form God reveals it, and hopefully steer clear of unhealthy ways of coping.

I believe that part of the work for all of us is to pay attention to the people around us who are grieving and to figure out how we can step in as the support structure they may need. If we are the ones grieving and can muster up the courage, we should try to receive people who want to give us a helping hand.

If we still find ourselves without a healthy support system and don't have access to professional therapy or counseling, there may be things from our childhood that can help us navigate our grief. Go all the way back to the beginning. I wouldn't have been able to connect the loss of my father with the loss of my son had I not been willing to dig a little into my past and uncover those feelings. Memories, lessons, and past experiences can provide anchors to help us through. This was especially true for me because, though my grandparents were gone, I still had the memories of how they moved through their grief and the lessons my grandma taught me.

I still hear her voice when I feel myself sinking into the darkness about Brandon's death. *"Keep living, Rickey. God is with you. You can make it."* When I hear this, I know that I can press on, that I can keep going.

When, in your past, have you either observed someone navigating grief well or were taught life lessons that could be useful now? Allow those thoughts and memories to ground you. Because that's really what any grieving person is longing for, aside from the return of their loved one.

Grief can be unmanageable. Unpredictable. It shows us our lack of control. We are being forced, it feels like, to surrender. I've had to reckon with the fact that I did not have any control over Brandon's death, and as a parent, that's one of the hardest things to accept.

Again, it's all hard. The feeling of being out of control that grief brings can cause us to spiral. There's no doubt about that. But if you do the work of building a village of support the best you can, I firmly believe God will be there with you, helping you move through grief in the way that *you* need to. Grief is individualized, so no matter how many words I write in this book, my process won't look like yours. How I move through my loss and the issues I encounter as I move through it will be different from the way you do it. But we can learn from each other's grief processes, gathering nuggets here and there to help us through.

This is an important point. Even as we form community and support each other through grief, it's important not to make the mistake of thinking that another person's grief has to look like ours. We're all just trying to get through. And again, it's challenging—actually the greatest work of my life. But as long as I hold on to the belief that God is there and present, I think I am better off holding on to my faith than relinquishing it and dealing with this unwieldy set of emotions with nothing to hold me, nothing to anchor me in place. I know I'm better off with God in my life. As I said, I don't judge anyone who doesn't feel that way. But if you're wondering how I got over—how I'm getting over—as Aretha Franklin sang,[2] it's because of God. I could have walked away from my faith. I could have decided that God was responsible for Brandon's death and never prayed or praised again. But I don't believe that. God has been present with me through it all. He has sat with me in this grief and kept me from going off the deep end. It is God who has made me resilient. It is God who continues to light my way.

But it was also my family who, whether through songs or sermons, blessed me with access to the light. The five great-grandparents I was fortunate enough to meet brought me to it, and they still haunt my dreams in a good way. Their love is still present. Only there is now one more among them: Brandon. I suppose they all, including my son, are passing me the aux cord of wisdom and healing now. I just hope I can hear the music.

3

ROASTING AND REPAIR

We can be.
Be and be better.
For they existed.
—MAYA ANGELOU

THERE WAS NOTHING SPECTACULAR ABOUT MY EARLY years in school. I went to Anna Stuart Dupuy Elementary on Fourteenth Avenue, then North Roebuck Elementary on Red Lane, and pretty much did what I was supposed to do. I often wonder if the reason I don't remember much about that time is because I lost my dad when I was in first grade. I can't say for sure, but it's something I've thought about. I also imagine that my home life was so rich with love and activity that I never really considered school a thing to love or hate. It simply was what it was. I didn't get into much trouble early on, and those years passed quickly.

The shift came around fifth grade—about the same time most children enter adolescence and start trying to figure out who their friends are and how they want to show up in the world. During this time, I wasn't as attentive to my schoolwork as I probably should have been. I was, however, figuring out how much I loved to laugh. I wasn't quite the jokester yet. There were other kids I ran with who were funnier than me. I was the "laugher." I would crack up laughing at anything and everything, and my loud silliness alone would get other folks going. But by sixth grade, the comedian in me was born. My friends and I loved to roast each other. It never failed that, by the end of the school day, we'd end up laughing until we almost passed out at some crazy "your mama so . . ." joke. Them dozens got played every day.

You want to know who was the greatest comedian with the best roasts in my sixth-grade classroom?

Our teacher, Ms. Alene Avery.

This woman was mean . . . and funny as hell. That's why we called her mean-funny. She could roast a kid and make us all lose it.

"That's why your mammy didn't give birth to you; she bought you, little boy!" she'd say to some kid who was acting out. The class would be completely wiped out, laughing.

"Hey, come here! What made you get up and not comb your hair? Take your tail in there and go comb that head. Don't come back in here without your hair combed."

I promise, my eleven-year-old self laughed so hard, tears flowed down my face. It was the first time that ever happened to me, and I was so confused. *Am I laughing so hard I'm crying?!*

Clearly, a teacher couldn't get away with this nowadays. We

know a bit more about the way children internalize hurtful words and how it impacts them. Parents are more sensitive and aware when it comes to how their children are treated. But honestly, I don't blame Ms. Avery one bit for coming for us. She was a good teacher who cared about every single one of us, but we also were a mess most of the time, and I'm sure we drove her up a wall most days.

There were two sixth-grade classes in our school. There was the honors classroom with all the high test scores and good study habits. And there was us. We were the hoodlums. And they put the hoodlums with the teacher who knew how to get us to learn. That's all that really mattered. So it probably made all the sense in the world at the time for her to get down on the level of a preteen boy or girl who just recently learned how to be slick in the mouth and tell them about themselves. I bet they didn't try whatever it was they did again. And there's only so many funky armpits and unkempt ponytails and Afros a person can take.

At the end of the term, our test scores came back higher than they'd ever been. Sure, she cussed us out. Yes, she dared us to go tell our mamas what she said about us. "Your mama ain't gonna do a damn thing." But she also made learning fun. Her roasting us, and us roasting each other, also made me think that being funny was a thing I could do. And best believe, I carried those roasting skills and my big laugh right on to summer school.

Because Lord have mercy, Little Rickey was *still* not doing his work.

Everybody got roasted in summer school. And afterward, when we'd all end up at the neighborhood park, the roasts got hotter. These guys were really funny, and I'm sure people heard my big

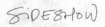

laugh all the way down the block. There was one older guy I grew up with who played the organ at church, but if you were ever shooting basketball with him, Derrick would roast you within an inch of your life. A church musician *and* funny? Man, I idolized this dude. Watching him, I knew I could be exactly who I ended up being: a musically inclined comedian who knows God.

Ain't none of that a contradiction either.

The one thing I'll always be grateful for is how God did not allow all the grief I've experienced in my life to take me off track of my purpose. I never stopped loving music. My love of music only amplified after the loss of my father. I never stopped telling jokes and being a comedian. The loss of my grandparents and great-grandparents, one by one over the years, only amplified my need for and desire to give the medicine that is laughter. And the loss of my son has not stopped me from knowing and trusting God, though there are days when it seems like it might.

When my granddaddy and grandmother passed away, it was hard to sit on that front pew at the funerals and not think about them sitting there only decades before, burying their son. The images of their pain were etched into my memory. Only I wasn't six years old anymore. I was in my thirties, and it was now one of them in the casket. But even when I thought I might sink into the black hole of my grief, it was music and comedy that saved me.

When I got the news about my grandmother passing, I was hosting BET's *Comic View* and doing a lot of promotional work for the show. I got the phone call just as I was getting ready to go onstage with AJ and Free, hosts of BET's music video show, *106 & Park*. Brandon and my nephew, Ron, were there with me on set because they loved traveling with me. After I hung up, I went out on the stage and did my thing. I used the laughter to quell the pain of loss I most certainly felt in my chest.

Something similar happened a few years before, when my other grandmother, my mom's mom, died. I was doing a show in Dothan, Alabama, that night. It was the same thing. I got the news and then went right onstage and did a whole set.

I got the call on my cell about my granddaddy dying just before legendary comedian Martin Lawrence was about to introduce me to perform in a show in New Orleans. And I did what I always did. I sucked it up, went onstage, and performed my butt off. In fact, I had a show in Jackson, Mississippi, the night of Granddaddy's funeral in Alabama. I went to the services and the repast and then jumped in a van and rode all the way to Jackson for the next show. Martin was so cool about all of it. When the news came out that my grandfather, who'd appeared on my reality show *Rickey Smiley For Real*, had passed away, Martin came down the hall and stuck his head in the door of my dressing room.

"Rick, you good?" he asked.

"Yes. Yes, I'm good, man. Thank you for the opportunity."

I respected Martin and his team. He was and is an icon in my eyes. There was no way I was going to let him or my granddaddy down that night.

You see, my grandfather would have wanted me on that stage. His work ethic was strong, and he expected that of me too. All of them did. When Big Mama, my great-grandmother, passed, my grandmother wouldn't let me come to the funeral because she knew I had an opportunity to open for Bernie Mac and DL Hughley in Columbia, South Carolina.

"Now, Rickey. Go to the funeral home to pay your respects, but Saturday, if I see you in that church at the funeral, we're going to have a problem, you hear?"

"Yes, ma'am," I said.

"You go do your show," she continued. "Mama is gone, and she would want you to go do your show. That's a big opportunity. You do your show and do not come to that funeral."

I did exactly what she told me to do. I drove an Oldsmobile Cutlass Supreme to Columbia, South Carolina, and opened for Bernie Mac and DL Hughley at the Township Auditorium.

I had a job to do. My people didn't believe in sitting around. They believed in getting back to the business of living. I'd watched them do it all my life, so when it was my turn, that's what came naturally. When tragedy or trauma comes, we handle it. But now that I'm on the other side of some of my greatest losses, I don't believe my grandparents and great-grandparents were teaching me to push my grief down so I didn't feel it. No, I don't think that was their lesson at all, although I'm sure there have been days, months, and even years when I did exactly that. When I didn't allow myself to feel too much, it was because the pain would make living unbearable. But that was me missing the point, I think. I was supposed to feel. I certainly get to decide when I would let my emotions overtake me, as I did in the early days after Brandon passed, but feeling them was absolutely necessary.

The lesson I think my grandparents were teaching me, the lesson life taught me, is that, as humans, we are built to be able to hold both grief and joy at the same time. I can cry my eyes out about missing Brandon only a few minutes before I hit the stage to tape my stand-up show and still go out there and make people laugh. And that's okay.

The truth is that all of us who are grieving need to take the time to feel what we feel. There's only so much numbing we can do before it begins to rot our insides, leaving us hollow and empty. Sometimes we must surrender to the pain, letting it wash over us like a cleansing rain. Sometimes we must release it. Let it out. Even when we aren't sure how to do that. We can absolutely be strategic about when, where, and how we express our emotions, but at some point, we have to allow ourselves the space to feel.

What many people forget, especially Black folks, is that we have been masters at holding both grief and joy simultaneously. We have demonstrated a remarkable resilience in the face of adversity. As a collective, we've held both pain and laughter for generations, so we certainly have the capacity to do it for ourselves individually. But some of us have forgotten that, I think. Some of us believe that if we are grieving, we should not experience joy. That to honor our lost loved ones, we cannot allow ourselves to be happy at all. We're taught to believe that in times of mourning, laughter and happiness have no place. But this couldn't be further from the truth. In fact, it's in the moments of laughter and joy that we find solace and healing.

As a matter of fact, if we're truly trying to heal from the pain of our grief, we are going to have to open ourselves up to joy. We're going to have to find time to feel the full gamut of emotions, not just sorrow or rage. I've watched people throughout my life, especially my grandparents and great-grandparents, do exactly that. I mean, think about it: When you go to a homegoing service, there is plenty of sorrow to go around. There's an undeniable heaviness that hangs in the air. There might be the great-auntie who wants to jump into the casket with the person, as well as other shenanigans that are bound to happen when family gathers. But there's also laughter. There are people sharing stories of the good times when the deceased made them laugh or was happy. There are hugs, kisses, and lots of love permeating the space even when great grief is present.

So when we try to formalize our grief and make it so that we can't feel anything else, it's not honoring. It's not a way of showing respect to the dead. In fact, by clinging to the notion that to laugh in the face of death is somehow disrespectful or dishonorable, we might be narrowing our loved one's legacy, their memory, because we are focusing only on the fact that they died and not on the fact that they lived. We are disregarding what their life brought to their community and maybe even the world. In the midst of the darkness of grief, there can be glimmers of light—a light born from the memories of joy and laughter shared with those we've lost.

There are so many moments with Brandon I choose to actively remember. Times when we laughed on the boat or in the car. When he sent me something funny in a text or we said "I love you" to each other. Those memories matter just as much as any wrestling I might have about the way he died. They matter just as much as my rage and sorrow at his death, if not more. So, I honor his memory not just by expressing my grief and anger but also by smiling at the time we were in the kitchen and I was teaching him how to cook a dish we loved. I can't stress enough how it is equally, if not more, important to maintain a balance of emotions as you go through the grief process. Please, give yourself permission to laugh.

As a comedian, part of what I do is try to help folks out in that regard, because I've witnessed the healing effect laughter can have on the human spirit. I want to give folks the permission they might need to laugh, even if it's just for the two hours they're sitting in an auditorium listening to me tell jokes. Because I know that laughter is medicine. I know that laughter will release something in their bodies that will make it easier when they're crying later on. I think that's what good memories and laughter do for us. It's more than just a temporary reprieve from the pain—it can be a lifeline if we let it. Joy can make it easier to handle other emotions like anger and frustration when they arise because we have allowed joy to soothe us in the meantime. That ability to hold joy takes the edge off the grief. It might even make grief not as prickly. It doesn't mean that grief won't rear its ugly head—sometimes at the worst time. It doesn't mean that grief isn't still painful. But if we allow ourselves to laugh or be happy in certain moments, then when grief does come, I like to think it's not as harsh.

We know from science that you can grieve to the point where you literally make your heart stop. There is a study from Rice University about how grief can cause inflammation in the body, which can cause diseases that ultimately can kill you.[1] We've heard the stories of couples who've been together for fifty years, and when one partner passes away, the other follows soon after. People say, "Oh, they died of a broken heart." This is the power of grief. It can overwhelm your body's systems. That's very real. Which is why we must allow ourselves to experience a little bit of joy and love so that grief and rage don't fully consume us.

I try to be intentional about having joy and laughter in my life. As I mentioned, I can be laughing one minute and crying the next, but I am finally learning to accept and experience the full range of emotions available to me, and I encourage you to do the same. You don't have to compartmentalize your grief or your joy. You can allow all your emotions to flow freely and demand that those around you accept that this is the space you're in for this season. Normalize this way of being emotionally flexible so that you don't find yourself feeling like you must hold on to any one emotion—like anger or sadness—and ultimately end up hurting yourself or someone else with it. If I never feel and then release a variety of emotions, I know I can become overwhelmed by the harsher ones. And I know Brandon wouldn't want that for me.

4

SON OF BIRMINGHAM

The LORD is close to the brokenhearted and
saves those who are crushed in spirit.
—PSALM 34:18 NIV

THE VERY FIRST TIME I HIT THE STAGE TO DO STAND-UP was November 13, 1989. It was a comedy club on Birmingham's Green Springs Highway. The owner, Bruce Ayers, held an open mic night there every week, with only a couple of simple rules.

"You got five minutes," he'd say.

"Your jokes gotta be clean and original," he'd say.

That's all I needed to hear. I took the stage that first night with just two jokes and started my career as a comedian.

Was I good? Eh, maybe, maybe not. Who can really say?

I was young. And green. But every week I showed up to the stage, and every week I got better. Much better.

So good, in fact, that after four months, Bruce leveled me up.

"I'm going to put you on a weekend show. You're now a professional. You're going to be opening for Mark DeShera."

So that's what I did. After Mark, I opened for George Wallace. Then Carl Strong.

And I kept getting better.

Then I met this comedian out of Cleveland. He was older than me by ten years and had already been on the scene for a good while. He wasn't quite a headliner yet but was much further along than me when it came to getting gigs. He knew the business and would always offer me great advice and guidance throughout my career. This Cleveland comedian, Steve Harvey, ended up going on to do big things. And I'm grateful that he still gives me great advice and guidance about the business and life.

But starting out? It was mostly just me, my jokes, and some terrible anxiety.

You see, I might be a son of Birmingham *now*. People know and respect me *now*. But back then, I was basically just some nineteen-year-old Black kid trying to make white folks laugh.

Yep, you read that right.

I started out telling jokes to mostly white audiences.

Black comedy as we know it now, with defined audiences and space, hadn't exploded yet. It didn't pop for real until *Def Comedy Jam* put a lot of us on in the nineties. But in 1989, Black comedians took stand-up gigs whenever and wherever they could, and most of the time, those gigs were clubs with predominantly white audiences.

Occasionally there were Black comedy nights at these clubs. When Steve came through Birmingham, he'd often headline WENN night, a midnight comedy show hosted by the Black radio station by the same name, which was owned by Dr. A. G. Gaston. That first WENN night is when I experienced the electricity that Black folks bring to a show. We talk back to comedians. We vibe with them. We laugh louder and harder. We also boo louder and harder, so there's that. It was different.

If I'm honest, white audiences were much easier. The best jokes for those audiences were mostly just sarcasm. It wasn't about creating a character or persona or having a particular style. The stories were shorter, less drawn out. I could walk out to a white audience, do my set without ever taking the microphone out of the stand, and still get laughs. That's unheard of at Black shows. Especially in the South. Especially in Birmingham. I tried it one time when I opened for Ice Cube and Da Lench Mob, Too Short, the Geto Boys, and D-Nice in the early nineties. I stood in one place and never took the mic out. And I got promptly booed off the stage. I learned quickly that if I'm talking to Black people, I had to come with a different swag. I had to pop that mic off the stand, walk back to the curtain, then out to the audience again with confidence. For Black folks, the comedy show isn't a show, for real. Yes, I'm performing, but in that moment, I am also a griot. I am the storyteller. And nowadays, the show is a whole conversation.

When I was first learning the game, I could write very basic jokes and just build them into my routine. Soon, though, I learned the best laughs came from a combination of material I'd already written and on-the-spot dialogue with the audience. This was especially true when it came to Black audiences. I had to employ the lessons of my childhood and be able to crack a joke just as well

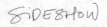

as I could tell one. In the beginning, though, I was finding my lane. I could write decent jokes, but that wasn't going to be enough to propel me anywhere. It was critical that I also figured out how to switch subjects smoothly or merge one joke into another. I had to decide when would be a good time to throw in a "Give it up for the ladies" or "Give it up to God" or ask the audience, "How many of y'all got kids?"

It flows now, but that's after thirty-five years of successes and failures. On November 13, 1989, I had none of the wisdom or experience of those years—just heart. My courage got me on that stage in my Jeans West outfit that I swore was casket sharp. Some friends came through. One was a guy who worked with me at a shoe store, Chester Porter (now a Bessemer, Alabama, city councilman). The guy who cut my hair, Doc, and his wife, Dot, who put in my Wave Nouveau, came through also. There was something about having my people in the audience, knowing someone was there to cheer me on.

One of the first lessons I learned about stand-up comedy was one I learned that very first night: it's less about the joke itself and more about your delivery of the joke. There is such a thing as stock jokes. Basic A + B = C jokes that nearly every comedian tells in some way, shape, or form. They aren't something you write but are more of a basic joke that everyone tells from a proverbial stock of jokes people have told over the years. It's very similar to the boy-meets-girl, boy-loses-girl, boy-does-the-most-to-get-girl-back formula that's common in most rom-com movies. No one really cares that it's the same premise from movie to movie; it's about *how* a movie tells that story. *Love & Basketball* is still different from *Love Jones*, which is very different from *Love Actually.* So in comedy, if I can take a stock joke that has a basic premise and deliver it uniquely, with my own style, and through the lens of my own lived experience, that joke becomes mine. And that's what I did that night. I was new to the stage, so I took a couple of stock jokes, made them relatable, and got laughs. Then I started writing my own—because I saw the funny in everything—and kept showing up every week to try stuff out.

After a few years of doing open mics, I started to become known around Birmingham. People called me to do all kinds of events, and I learned pretty quickly that I could make money doing this thing I loved so much. I also learned that I could make more money and become even more known if I hosted comedy shows too. I'd watched Steve and George and the others. I saw how the more they hosted, the more headliner gigs they'd get. I think it's mostly because hosting helps you with your timing as a comedian. You have to multitask by giving the announcements ("Y'all make sure you tip your waiters"), introducing the acts ("Coming next to the stage . . ."), and doing all this while weaving your own jokes in between. You're also forced to interact with the audience more because you're carrying the show's energy and keeping a flow going. This helps your timing and rhythm—something I picked up pretty quickly.

Those first few years on the Birmingham scene were a defining season for me. It's why I can honestly say the trajectory of my career has only been up. I've had some plateaus, but hardly any dips. I went from open mics in that nightclub to touring to *Comic View* and *Def Comedy Jam*, the latter being the pinnacle of "making it" for a Black comedian. After I went on *Def Comedy Jam*, I stayed working and never stopped. I did tours at clubs and colleges all around the country. I opened for Cedric the Entertainer before he blew up. I did Uptown Comedy Club, Showtime at the Apollo, and Comedy Central. I went on to do movies and more TV, including my own show. The bottom line is, I've kept the same courage that got me on the open mic stage that first night, and I have always been willing to learn and grow as a performer. Because of this, my ticket sales have been consistent since '97.

Radio came later. It has been the one area where I don't just make people laugh in the morning but also have a platform to share the fullness of who I am. That musical side of me gets just as much play. The part of me that's concerned about politics and the social issues plaguing my people, this country, and the world gets a say. The side of Rickey Smiley that must grieve in public also has a voice.

People have asked me if I've made my experience with grief and loss part of my stand-up show. I haven't yet. Only because I can't find much funny in it right now. I may mention Brandon at the end of the show and thank the audience for their prayers, but I haven't been able to incorporate any of this into the show.

But the shift in my work is still a real thing. I feel called to the grief-stricken. It's a kind of ministry now. I was doing karaoke one night at a club when an older woman in her sixties came up to me and held my hand.

"Won't you walk me to my car?" she asked.

I said, "Yes, ma'am."

When we got outside in the cold, she said, "I buried my son two weeks after Brandon died. Found him in the car. He had smoked some weed laced with fentanyl and that was it."

Whew! Her story hit me hard because I knew exactly how she was feeling, and I told her as much. I had no advice though. Since it had only been a short time since I'd lost Brandon, my pain was as fresh as hers. We were both feeling lost in a forest of grief, and so all we could do was hold each other in that parking lot and give each other space to feel what we feel.

I suppose I'm still like my grandfather in that way. Yes, I must grieve. I must take care of myself. But I also have a job to do. To whom much is given, much is required. I get on the radio every day and in some way, shape, or form, I let people know that God is real. I tell people to get out and vote, to elect the change they want to see in their communities, in this country. I ask people to consider not taking drugs that will take their life. I implore fathers to be better fathers and mothers to be better mothers. I try to help get folks elected. Again, if I can use my platform to make everybody's quality of life better, whether it's through laughter or activism, that's what I'm going to do. That's what I'm called to do. That's what my son would have wanted me to do.

I started in radio at a brand-new Birmingham station, WBHJ 95.7 Jamz. They needed a comedian for the *Buck Wilde Morning Show*, so my friend, Corey White, took me down to meet Mickey Johnson, the program director, and David Dubose, the GM. I landed the gig immediately. From there, I moved on to the *Doug Banks Morning Show* as a recurring comedian before getting fired for clashing with one of the producers. (That's another story for another book.) Finally, an opportunity of a lifetime came my way. My friend and mentor Steve Harvey, whose radio show had seen astronomical success, was moving from Radio One, the syndicator of his morning show, to Clear Channel. When they asked him who he'd recommend for a new morning show in Dallas, he told them, "Get Rickey Smiley. He's clean. He has political and spiritual awareness. And he's disciplined. He's going to get up and go to work every day."

That was it. I've been getting up at 3 a.m. every weekday for the last few years to host the *Rickey Smiley Morning Show*. Alfred Liggins, the CEO of Radio One, told me that if I beat the competition in Dallas, which at the time was K104, he'd offer me a syndication deal. When I did that, he personally went to Oklahoma to expand the show there. Then I aired in Miami and the show blew up. I am now Steve's competitor, but you know what? It's still all love between us. Sure, if we get into a room together, I'm going to mess with him because, hey, I'm an instigator. I'm gonna crack a *Family Feud* joke or say he gets his suits off the rack at Men's Warehouse. But I'm only trash-talking and button-pressing someone I deeply love and respect. Steve will always be my brother, fraternal and otherwise.

And now I get to do for others what Steve did for me. I get to take Corey Holcomb, Loni Love, Flame Monroe, and Nephew Tommy on the road with me. I get to work with Da Brat, Gary With Da Tea, Special K, Rock-T, and Maria More daily.

The world of comedy is a hell of a ride. At least it has been for me. Yes, it's about making people laugh; but I think what I love even more is the ability to build relationships with and give back to the people who share the stage with me. Especially when they are younger and coming up in this business. I have a great bond with B. Simone. We have a real connection, and she's very coachable. There have absolutely been times when I've pulled her to the side, got in her face about something or another, and then watched her go out and nail it onstage. And guess who was standing on the side of the stage jumping up and down, screaming like a proud dad? Yep, me. In real time, I got a chance to see her take my direction, heed it, and get better results. And when she came offstage, we high-fived each other with tears in our eyes. I kept saying, "What did I tell you?" The pride I felt in my chest was overwhelming. It was like I was a comedy dad cheering on one of his kids.

So naw, I'm not *always* the old head yelling the proverbial "get off my lawn" and complaining about the youngins. I can clearly see a generational shift happening in comedy. The internet's best are taking the stage, and I'm grateful I can do my small part in guiding some of them. Comedians like DC Young Fly, whom I see as a nephew. Desi Banks, who has gone from online success to live shows in a much shorter time than any of us old heads could have. I ain't mad at none of it. At all. I put Desi on the stage in Birmingham— now he's selling out shows everywhere. I can't even begin to say how good that feels. So yeah, critics can say what they want, but these young talents have figured out where the audience is—online—and they are capitalizing on that.

But I have love for the OGs too. The people who came up before me, with me, or right after me. I have a great respect and love for

Mike Epps, Earthquake, Lavell, Bruce Bruce, Arnez J, DeRay Davis, and yes, Katt Williams too (more on that much later). It's these guys who paved the way for the kids who are coming up now.

After being on the radio for more than fifteen years, I'm often asked about getting back into TV or film. While I'm not ever going to have a closed mind about any opportunity, at this stage of my life, I'm considering more than just what will give me more, more, more. In truth, radio pays me more than any TV show I ever did. It's given me more social media followers than I had viewers on TV. The schedule I have in radio affords me the kind of rest I need in order to work on myself. By getting up at 3 a.m., my workday is over by 9:30 a.m. if I don't have meetings or shows. This gives me time to sit with myself. To meet with my therapist. To heal from the big, Brandon-shaped hole in my chest. So why exactly would I chase after something that doesn't align with what I enjoy or need?

Right now, family is crucial to me. It's what matters the most. And I mean *all* my family—not just my blood kin. The morning show crew? Fellow comedians? They're my family. The B. Simones and Desi Bankses in my life? They check up on me like family does. I care for them like family should.

There was a time when I was hyperfocused on my career, and of course there are things I still want to do. But nowadays I can't help but think more about taking my grandkids to the beach or pushing them on the swings. I love cooking some pinto beans and greens or some chicken and dumplings and watching them eat with big ol' smiles on their faces. I'm always going to choose those things over sitting in some damn trailer memorizing a script. I can't stand doing that. It drives me crazy. And those trailers might look sophisticated on TV, but they aren't ever balanced. You are either leaning one way about to fall off the couch or leaning the other way and unable to get your butt up off the couch. I know there are some nice trailers out there, but I still don't like how they look, feel, or smell. The last movie I was in, *Miracles Across 125th Street* with Nick Cannon, I went without a trailer altogether. I brought my Mercedes Sprinter to set, backed it in, plugged it up, and was so much more comfortable.

I know this is counter to all the stuff people put out there about grinding and hustling. And I do believe there is a season for all of us to bust our tails, work hard, and build our careers. But there are also seasons when we need more balance. I love going to shoot something like the sketch comedy and game show *Wild 'N Out* for the day. I have my fun, but I also get in and get out. I do this because I've learned over the years that, at some point, we all have to keep the main thing the main thing. For me, that looks like spreading the work out. I think of some people in the business whom I love and respect and who are doing amazing things. But I often ask myself, *Does she even sleep? Does he have time for his kids?* Losing a child will absolutely force you to put all that into perspective.

This reminds me of an observation I made after watching LeBron James play basketball. It's about taking shots in basketball. The key to making a shot is stepping back to create some space before you shoot. And it's the same in life, I think. Sometimes in the midst of all the hustle and bustle, you have to take a step back, create space, and then take your shot. And that might mean you whittle down your entourage. It might mean you love folks from a distance, not having folks in your face all the time. Nowadays, I

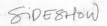

don't even like to have a bunch of people backstage with me before a show. Because tending to them becomes an extra job. Boundaries are more important than ever.

Since Brandon passed, and maybe even starting a few years before, I've learned so much about setting boundaries even when my heart doesn't want to. Setting boundaries is crucial. It's like traffic lights—if everyone did whatever they wanted on the road, we'd have pure chaos.

People ask me to do stuff all the time. Especially when I'm home in Birmingham. When they do, my question is simple: What comes with what you're asking? You want me over for dinner? Cool, but does that mean I have to be friends with your daughter's friend's parents who are invited? Will they want to exchange numbers? Okay, well that might be a lot for me right now. Again, I'm the only one responsible for my mental and emotional health. And while I will always engage my people—and Lord knows I do—I have to be careful that I'm not being required to engage my people's people's people. Because that can get heavy.

There was one time when I was offered a large sum of money to flip a coin at an HBCU game. Sounds easy, right? Maybe. But there's always more to it. I have to walk through the crowd. In that crowd will likely be people who will want pictures and people who will want to heckle and cuss me out. Sure, it's money in the bank, and in a different season of life, it might be something worth doing. But now, knowing what I know about how short life is, I always ask myself, *Is it worth the mental stress?* And most of the time, the answer is no. I'd rather keep my peace.

So no, I won't be the grand marshal at that parade or flip a coin at that game if it means compromising my mental health. All money isn't good money, and I'd rather have respect than be liked. I'm a kind person, sure, but the reality is that while a lot of people have good motives, other people will try to take advantage of you if you allow it. It's the nature of the beast, especially in this business. Some folks see kindness and think, *Let's see how much we can get from him.* And that's when I have to correct people. There's nothing wrong with being direct. For saying exactly what you need and how you feel. I've been known to say to a person, "No, I do not want to do that" or "Do not say that to me." Braces hurt, but they correct a smile. Same with correction—it might sting, they might be momentarily stunned that you dared speak up for yourself, but it sets things right.

Of course, I say all that knowing I'm nowhere near perfect. Sometimes *I* need correction too. Sometimes I need to know when I've crossed a boundary. Because I know this, I've also never been afraid to receive correction—when it's warranted and necessary. If Steve Harvey or DL Hughley or George Wallace got on me about something I did that was dead wrong, do you know what my answer would be?

"Yes, sir."

That's it.

One time I was on the radio and Tom Joyner, who was also with Radio One in the same city, heard me do or say something completely out of pocket—I cannot even remember what it was. Do y'all know that Tom drove down to my station in Dallas's Valley View Mall and cussed me straight out? And again, what was my response?

"Yes, sir."

I didn't offer an explanation. I didn't justify my actions. I took it, because if this brother who has no dog in the ring of my career cared enough about me to come and cuss me out in order to get me back on the right path, I was going to listen to every word he said. I was going to, as the Nat King Cole song says, "straighten up and fly right."[1]

Correction and setting boundaries with family are also necessary. With my kids, biological or not, I've had to lay down the law at times. Because I've learned the hard way what happens when you don't. The grief journey I'm on isn't *just* about the tears and the pain and the trauma. It's also about what I've learned. How I'm growing through it all. It's teaching me how to be true to myself. It's teaching me how and when to, like LeBron, take a step back and create space when I need it.

When you're grieving, it's really easy to just keep moving. To keep working. It's too tempting to immerse ourselves in ceaseless activity, burying our emotions beneath layers of busyness. Maybe we think that if we just keep going, we won't have to think about the grief and sorrow that awaits us. We try to play emotional dodgeball with grief, hoping we can get away from its fierce throws by not allowing ourselves a moment to stop and feel anything. People who have been shattered by the blow of loss might find some form of solace in perpetual motion. They might try to outrun grief. But I know from my own experience and from observing other grievers that nine times out of ten, those of us who have experienced a significant loss in our lives and who have responded to that loss with constant movement and work are usually the ones who are in the deepest pain. We are also the ones likely headed toward a huge implosion of grief in our bodies. Because what we all soon learn, when we stop running around, is that the sorrow remains.

We must create some space for ourselves in the grieving process. We also need more balance in our lives. To be honest, I wasn't a proponent of this idea a decade ago. I was all about the hustle and grind. I once believed that success was about making a certain amount of money or having a certain kind of notoriety. That's the world we live in. Success is often wrongly measured in terms of accomplishments and accolades. And I do still believe that you must work hard for the things you want. But I also know that there comes a time when you have to realize that there are other things that matter. That family matters. That taking care of yourself matters. And if that's true, then you do have to stop and think about that grief. It's in your best interest to take a minute or a month to rest—whatever you can manage—and give yourself space to breathe. It is a way to heal, especially when you've experienced heavy loss.

Creating space for grief is not a sign of weakness but rather an act of courage. It requires us to confront the pain that lies dormant within us, to sit with it, to hold it close, even as it threatens to overwhelm us. But it's not just about dealing with pain. It's also about finding balance. It's about recognizing that our worth is not defined by our productivity. We need to have moments when we can be still. We need time for rest and to gain perspective.

Part of my love of boating is that being in my boat gives me time to just be still. To sit and watch the sun set or rise over the ocean. It offers me some often much-needed perspective. You can't take a boat ride and not realize just how small we all are. That there's bigger and greater out there. That there's a God who knows more than we do. It gives me peace. It is also a kind of rest I give to my mind, body, and spirit.

I get the same feeling when I'm with my family. Especially my children and grandbabies. When I get to hug and kiss and love on them, I'm reminded that they are more important than all the hands I get to shake or all the celebrities I get to talk to. Don't get me wrong. I love my work, and I love what I get to do and how I get to do it. I love the people I get to meet. I'm grateful for so many of those individuals I have been able to establish friendships with and who I likely would not have met had I not been called to this work. But that is only a small portion of what gives me joy.

My work cannot be the only thing that offers me happiness, because it's still work. I don't care what you do; your job can wear on you. Especially in the entertainment business where so much of what we see is tainted by evil, not-well-intentioned people. People who want to take advantage of your talent or the audience you've built because they see it as profitable but have no intention of sharing that profit with you. People whose personal agendas can often override the creation of good art. And so in addition to making people laugh, I'm tasked with watching my back. I'm constantly mindful about not becoming so consumed by one part of my world that I don't allow myself some harmony or some balance.

So choose what that looks like for you. Your way of creating space and having balance might be spending time with your family. It might be gardening. It might be watching movies or vegging out on the couch to watch your favorite reality television show. What will allow your brain to rest? What's going to allow your spirit to be surrounded by the warmth of comfort? And are you willing to be still long enough to do any of these things?

I'm one of the grieving people who tends to keep moving to stay busy. Some grieving people keep moving because it makes them feel like they have something of value to offer. We can all find ourselves questioning our purpose and importance in this world when we lose someone we love. Grief can make you wonder why you are even here. It can make you feel that you somehow don't have a purpose. So you start trying to reclaim your significance by doing too much when, actually, you're being called to a season of stillness and rest in order to heal whatever has been triggered by your loss.

Sure, there might be a time when you must keep moving. There might be a season when you have to focus on putting your loved one's affairs in order, preparing for the ceremonies, taking care of family members who can't take care of themselves, that kind of thing. But as I myself came to learn, you are eventually going to have to build in some time to just sit with yourself, take in what has happened, and pray for God to send a healing balm to your heart to repair what might have been broken by the loss of your loved one.

So yes, I get why we keep going. I do. Like I said, at my father's funeral, I watched my grandfather keep moving until he couldn't anymore. But perhaps that was the lesson for me. For us. We have the choice to be more intentional about creating some room for ourselves during our grieving process. That way, when we do return to the stream of life, we're stronger. We can operate in true purpose and not a manufactured one.

Despite going back to work on my radio show fairly quickly, I know the space I did take for myself in the aftermath of Brandon's death, the time I took off on my boat or gathered my family, made me stronger in the long run. That's what rest is supposed to do, right? That's what creating space helps us do. We can step back and see what's going on around us so the next decision we make, whether it's for work or anything else, is more intentional and more in alignment with what God has for us.

Here's the thing: I know how blessed I am. Most people don't have the kind of career trajectory I've been fortunate to have. Especially fifty-five-year-old Black men from Birmingham, Alabama. And even if they do, being in the entertainment business often means that opportunities can dry up just as quickly as they appear. So to have a job that doesn't feel like a job, where I get to have fun and be completely myself every day? Well, I know that's nothing but God at work.

When this son of Birmingham surrendered to being a giver above and beyond anything else, when I created space and more balance in my life, when I gave in to the realization that anything coming *to* me is actually coming *through* me, and that it's up to me to turn my blessings into more blessings for others, I think that's when God started trusting me with this life I have. Lately, though, it's been the challenge of my life to reconcile all that favor with the devastations I've experienced in my family. Especially the loss of my son. This looks like it will be the next stop on my grief journey, and it's far from over.

PART TWO

I AM A FATHER

Above all, keep loving one another earnestly,
since love covers a multitude of sins.
1 Peter 4:8

5

BECOMING A DAD

When you are sorrowful look again in your heart, and you shall see that in truth you are weeping for that which has been your delight.
—KAHLIL GIBRAN

I KNOW WHAT THE COMMON PERCEPTION IS OF A father who has a career like mine. A stand-up comedian with four children couldn't possibly be an active part of their lives, right? Yet I'm so grateful this wasn't and isn't my story. For a large part of my career, I mostly performed on weekends. Shows were generally Friday and Saturday nights, and the remaining time was used for travel back and forth. Since radio wasn't in the picture in those early years, my weekdays were always reserved for being the dad who walked his kids to the bus stop. The one who made sure they had what they needed for school and any extracurriculars.

When the kids got older and I had weekend shows, I would often bring them with me. Make it a road trip. Miami meant a beach day, Orlando led to Disney, Tampa took us to Busch Gardens, and Louisville introduced us to Kentucky Kingdom. Stand-up roller coasters were Brandon's and my thing, and I have so many pictures of us with our mouths open or faces twisted while riding those rides. Those were the best days. He loved me, and I loved him.

Brandon, being the oldest, was rarely far away from me, even though his mom and I had long been broken up. Brenda and I met on a school bus back in high school. I was a senior at Woodlawn High School, and she was this cute freshman who was on the volleyball team. My friend fixed us up with each other, and we started dating pretty quickly. We had five years of an on-again, off-again relationship that was filled with the typical teenage drama—other boys, other girls, misunderstandings. It also didn't help that my comedy career had taken off, and suddenly there were women all around me. We broke up after she had Brandon in 1990 and before she finished high school. She eventually met her husband there, who became a great bonus father to Brandon. In the meantime, I continued chasing my dreams to become an entertainer.

Regardless of us not being together, the greatest gift I was given from our time together was my boy, Brandon. I was so overwhelmed the first time I saw his little face. He was a beautiful baby. Sadly, I couldn't be at the hospital when she delivered him, but when I got to Brenda's house after she was discharged, I'll never forget walking in on the chaos of her trying to change his diaper after a major blowout. *Well, hello to you, too, son!*

Listen, when things got rough with me and Brenda's attempts to co-parent, I fought to see my boy. There was a season when Brenda and I stayed at the courthouse. Things got really ugly at one point because I felt like she was not willing to work with me in light of the work I did. There were times she was so resistant to the occasional switching of weekends to accommodate my schedule of being on the road. Because of this, I filed for a better custody agreement. I was never going to be cool with the standard visitation deal that's given to fathers by courts who have all these preconceived beliefs about how much time men, Black men especially, actually want to spend with their children. I was *not* the one. Even at twenty years old, with the career I had, I didn't want just forty-eight hours a month to be with my child. I wanted a reasonably equal amount of time, and I wasn't going to back down. Brandon knew my voice, of course, but I refused to be *just* a voice on the other end of the phone like my dad was for me. Being present matters.

I'm a firm believer that children need both parents, and I was very vocal about that. Through it all, I made it a point to be there. I was there when he took his first steps. Eventually, he came to live with me.

But even before he lived with me, my attitude had always been: *no matter the distance, no problem.* Even on the road, I often made sure Brandon was with me. Sometimes during my visitation weekends, I would hire someone to pick up Brandon in Atlanta where his mom and stepdad lived and bring him to wherever I was. Do you know how hard that was? Paying for someone to drive my child from Atlanta to wherever just so I could see his face? But it was worth every penny spent. In fact, Brandon became a fixture at my shows. His toys would be spread all around my dressing room, and

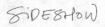

we were always pulling pranks on each other. Sometimes I even let him try his hand at telling jokes onstage. This undoubtedly played a role in him becoming a comedian himself as an adult.

Despite the sometimes-contentious custody battles, Brenda and I both wanted what we thought was best for Brandon. I knew that. We loved him. And that love ultimately allowed for things to smooth out a little as he got older. Brandon was a very carefree and content child. He rarely complained. He was always my guy, even when things took a turn in his later teenage years.

Our amusement park adventures around the country took off when he was around seven. We went to close to a hundred parks but never made it to the one at the top of our list: Cedar Point in Ohio. I was hoping that one day we'd get there. Nowadays, I just imagine us there. In my mind's eye, I see his face and mine in full-on joy. I see us riding the Corkscrew or the Gatekeeper, somehow, somewhere between my side of glory and his.

I think many parents who have lost a child to drug addiction often try to remember the moment when everything went left. We try to pinpoint the shift that turned our babies into someone we didn't recognize. I know I did. Brandon came to live with me in the ninth grade, and things were cool those first couple of years. But sometime around the eleventh grade, he started to change. It felt like one day we were this super close, pops-and-son duo, and then the next thing I knew, I was finding bongs and roach clips in his room. From that point on, Brandon's behavior got progressively worse. The innocent, bright-eyed little boy who used to grab my hand in the car and say "I love you!" had started wilding out. This, I think, was the critical moment when everything shifted, not just for him but for me as a father. But even then, I chalked it up to the kind of experimentation many teens get into as they are trying to figure themselves out.

I'm certain that Brandon's drug use escalated during his time in college—mostly due to partying and hanging with the wrong people. I didn't notice much at first. When he came home, everything seemed okay. But then his grades started to drop, so I took him out of Alabama State University and sent him to the University of Alabama. That's when I first started to notice the color of his lips getting darker. "You smoke cigarettes?" I'd ask. But he wouldn't really respond. I'd follow up with "So what else you smoking?" He still never gave a straight answer. It wasn't until later that I discovered the extent of his struggles. He'd begun dabbling in harder drugs—heroin, cocaine, and finally, opioids. Brandon ended up in trouble at the University of Alabama because of those same drugs. They arrested him for intent to distribute. I hired an attorney to help his case, but ultimately, Brandon was kicked out of school.

Like most dads would, I tried to intervene. The first thing I did was *strongly* encourage him to sign up for the National Guard, thinking the discipline and routine of service would help him get and stay clean. I remember crying so hard when I learned he could be sent to Afghanistan. That weekend, I was sitting in church when the choir started singing Clay Evans's song "For the Rest of My Life." The tears just flowed like a river. Then Monday came, and Brandon called me.

"I'm upset," he said.

SIDESHOW

"Why?" I asked.

"They canceled our order to go."

Relieved, I continued, "Okay, so why are you upset?"

"I was prepared to go," he said.

He was prepared to go. Those words echo in my mind now. At the time, I couldn't imagine what it would be like for him to go off to war and not come back. All I could think about was what war did to my dad. How could I have known that many years later I still would experience those exact feelings of loss?

The grace of God prevailed when the military canceled Brandon's order to go overseas and he eventually was discharged. But unfortunately, they couldn't cancel his attraction to drugs. Something was drawing him back to whatever it was those chemicals offered. Was it just a chemical dependence? Was it numbing? If so, what exactly did he not want to feel? Was it safety? If so, why didn't he feel safe? I know these are questions I will never have answers to, and yet I ask them anyway because part of this grief process has been to sit with that pain and then surrender it to God, who I believe does know all the answers.

There's absolutely a risk inherent in becoming a parent. So many uncertainties live alongside the joys. It marks a transition from individual to caregiver. With the decision to bring a child into the world comes a myriad of hopes, dreams, and fears. It's an act of courage and profound love but also a leap into the unknown. Two things are true: As parents, we get the privilege of watching our kids grow, learn, and flourish. But we also experience the ever-present fear of making mistakes and of failing our children in some fundamental way.

On the one hand, your child might absolutely adhere to everything you've taught them. They might listen to you and go off and do things based on whatever values and morals you instilled in them as a child. On the other hand, there's an equal chance that your child will not listen to you at all and go left when you say right or up when you say down. They might veer off course despite your best efforts. Despite your knowing that one mistake, one misstep—on their part or yours—could change the trajectory of their lives forever. It's all risky business, becoming a mother or a father or a parent. And yet so many of us do it anyway.

In having kids, we have essentially decided that the risk is worth it. We choose to love our children and we do the best we can for them, regardless of how they might receive it, regardless of what they ultimately do with it in their adult lives. In the end, we surrender control. That's been so hard for me. Because, for real, I'm the "do what I tell you to do and you'll be all right" type of dad. And what Brandon's loss has taught me is that I have to give up that control.

Yes, I can give the best advice. I can provide all the trappings of a comfortable life for my children. I can even provide resources for when they are in need or when they find themselves in trouble. I can do all that and still not have the power, once they become an adult, to make them take advantage of those resources, to make them listen, or to apply any value to what I say. And the hardest truth is, I might not always be right, at least from their perspective. As a father,

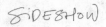

I've had to confront my own shortcomings, insecurities, and fears. Whew! You talk about hard to hear? It's hard to hold all of that, especially as a father with adult children.

It's easy to tell your five-year-old to go sit down somewhere and have the expectation that they will, in fact, go sit down somewhere. It is not so easy to tell your twenty-year-old they probably shouldn't be hanging with that group of people and then watch them completely ignore your guidance. You are bound to have a range of feelings when that happens. Lots of anger and frustration. Definitely sorrow, because you know what might happen to your child if things go wrong the way you fear they might. But that's part of the surrender. We must be willing to let go of our expectations and accept our children for who they are, not who we want them to be.

When I was coming up, many Black Baptist churches held baby dedication services. It was like the christenings in Catholic churches. At a baby dedication, parents bring their children to the front of the church and the pastor prays over them. The parents are dedicating their children to God in the same way Hannah dedicated the future prophet Samuel to God in 1 Samuel 1:21–28. In the moment of dedication, we are vowing to be our children's guide. To not only provide for them but to teach them how to live. We are also trusting that God will ultimately protect them. That He will lead them. Dedicating our babies also means trusting in the inherent goodness of God and believing that He is in control even when we don't understand His actions. We surrender our babies to God in that way. But the truth is, this dedication is a ceremonial act we usually do when our children are infants and can't fend for themselves—when they need us in every way possible. But what happens when that baby becomes an eighteen-, nineteen-, or twenty-year-old adult, or when that child is now thirty-two years old?

As parents, we try to do our part in dedicating our children to God—praying over them, guiding and providing for them. But as adults, they must do that work for themselves. And the hard truth is that some will, and some won't. If you are the parent who has the child who won't, if you're the parent who has the child who breaks your heart over and over again, surrendering your desire to control their outcomes can be a kind of grief before the grief. This has been the hard part for me: accepting that my child made choices as an adult that I had no control over. Every day I have to surrender that fact to God.

Could I have intervened in my son's downward spiral into addiction earlier? I suppose I could have, had I really known the depths of what was happening. I will forever wonder if something could have been done differently. But I also know that Solomon in Ecclesiastes 7:10 advised, "Do not say, 'Why were the old days better than these?' For it is not wise to ask such questions" (NIV). Therefore, I will hold tightly to the wisdom in accepting that I did my absolute best with what I knew and had.

I wish life gave us predictable, neat endings like the ones we see on TV. That's rarely the case, though. If you'd suggested as I was riding those roller coasters with a then six- or seven-year-old Brandon that I'd be mourning him twenty-five years later, I would have probably denied it and cussed you out for saying it. Yet here we are. I do know that all of us battle forces beyond our control. Brandon was no different. He could have stopped. Many people do.

He could have made a different choice. Many do. But the thread of addiction in his bloodline was likely one of those forces that proved too strong for him to overcome. That's also true for so many. If I haven't learned anything else, I know that parenting can reveal not just current issues, pains, and traumas that feel beyond our control, but it can also unearth the issues, pains, and traumas running through our families.

6

WHEN ADDICTION CHASES
THE BLOODLINE

If you don't transform the trauma, it gets transferred.
—Jerry Tello, National Compadres Network

MOST PEOPLE ARE SURPRISED WHEN I TELL THEM I'VE never smoked a joint. And except for a hot toddy when I'm sick or an occasional glass of wine with my steak, I don't drink. Which is strange, I know, when you consider the thread of addiction that exists in my family. I think there's a part of me that just knew not to go that route. Even in college, when friends wanted to get twisted before a party, or the Bruhs (a slang name for members of my fraternity, Omega Psi Phi Fraternity, Inc.) would make that special punch, I was never the one to indulge and was always the designated driver. I got teased for not drinking. My friends and frat would roast me, calling me Joe No Drink. Even when I'd pretend like I was going to drink a beer, they'd slap it so fast out my hand and say, "Nah, you ain't finna waste our beer. Put that down."

When I consider how I was able to avoid the pitfalls of addiction, it really does go back to my wonderful grandparents. It was as simple as them telling me, "Rickey, don't do it." That's all it took. And it wasn't like none of my grandparents drank or smoked. They did. I remember my grandmother telling me to light her cigarette on the gas stove and then, when I gave it to her, turning to me and saying, "Now, don't let me catch you smoking!" I know how to make fantastic drinks despite not drinking them because my granddaddy loved him a nice Crown and Coke and taught me how to make it just right. But as I unpack that duality, I now realize they weren't necessarily being hypocritical when they told me not to mess around with drugs or alcohol. It was what they *weren't* saying. The words behind the words that ultimately influenced me. "Rickey, don't do it" really meant "Rickey, we've been through this already. We've seen the pain alcoholism and drug abuse can cause. We've lived through the chaos and ultimate loss." They never went that deep with me, of course. But I felt it. I felt deep down in my bones that their "don't do it" was also a cry for me to not make them hurt like that again. So I didn't.

My dad had no such awareness. In fact, in many ways, I think he might have been born with a double dose of rebellion. I remember the stories of him being in Vietnam for the war but also learning to speak Vietnamese and play the drums. It was like he loved being a walking contradiction. My dad was a determined musician, and as much as my mother was a guiding force in my love for music, I've come to terms with the fact that I probably got a few things from him in that regard too. I play the piano, and he played the drums. He loved some good soul music, and so do I. He was also the life of the party—very funny—so I suppose I get that honestly too. But, as I've hinted, Dad had a darker side. When he returned from the war and moved to New York, my grandparents tried everything they could to pull him back home to Alabama. But he refused. It was like something was holding him and he couldn't release himself from the music but also from the drugs and street life that would swallow him whole in the end.

My grandmother, my mother's mother, once told me that she pointed her finger at my dad and said, "Baby, you got death on you." Old people in the South did that a lot. When somebody was living a certain lifestyle, the elders could see it coming from a mile away. Dad was hiding out with my mother's family because he was on the run from his own father. Granddaddy had gotten mad one day because Dad pushed my grandmother and then went to hide out at my other grandmother's house. He vowed to kill my dad and told him straight up that if he didn't turn his life around, "You going to leave here."

My uncle tried to warn Dad also. He shared with me how he sat in a New York City bar one evening with tears in his eyes, begging my dad to come home. But stubborn as ever, Dad chose a different path. Two weeks after my uncle returned from New York, my dad was dead. Everyone in our family feared Dad's resistance would be the thing that ended him. And I know intimately what that kind of fear feels like.

I, too, warned Brandon. Over and over and over again. Up until the end, when it wasn't looking good. Even on our reality show, there is footage of me tearing up while trying to get him to change. But he'd always blow it off.

"Yes, sir," he'd say.

"I'm straight, Dad," he'd try to convince me.

I even sat my other children, his siblings, down and warned them that if Brandon did not try to beat this thing, he would likely die from it. That day, I flew my daughter Aaryn home from college. I told Malik to drive home from college in Montgomery. D'Essence was already there in Birmingham.

"Y'all need to start preparing yourself," I said. "Brandon might not make it."

They'd just lost their cousin, my nephew Ron, to drugs, so I'm sure this wasn't something they wanted to hear from me. But I knew they *needed* to hear it. "If Brandon don't get clean after seeing what happened to Ron," I continued, "he can die from this. I just want to put y'all on notice that this can happen." That's when they all started crying.

"Why do you say that?!" they all asked.

"Because of what he's doing! Because of what's out there!"

I think they knew what I was saying was true. Ron, my nephew, had died. My pastor's daughter had died. Ironically, they were both thirty-two like Brandon was when they passed.

"He's sick, and it's not looking good," I said finally.

The Wednesday after Brandon passed away, Malik walked in the kitchen where I was sitting by myself. "Dad, I was at Brandon's on Christmas. For some reason when I left, I knew it was going to be my last time seeing him," he said. "You called it."

"I know," I said.

Like my grandmother before me, I did know. But I really wish I didn't.

I know how all this sounds. It's kind of harsh to tell your children that their brother is going to die. But I couldn't help but feel the weight of history. I warned them, just as my grandmother had warned my dad, about the possibility of death because I know what that anticipation of the inevitable feels like. And still, I hate that my words feel prophetic now.

How do you prepare for the possibility of your child dying while still hoping they choose life? When I sat down with my children and essentially gave them the heads-up that, based on the way their brother was living, it was a possibility he wouldn't be here much longer, I hoped I was off base, that somehow there would be an intervention that could work. I always held on to a sense that maybe he would arrive at the conclusion that he wanted more for his life, that he wanted more for himself without me necessarily always being in his ear, trying to tell him what to do. But there was this other clear part of me that had seen too much, knew too much. The part that had lived long enough to see countless people, from acquaintances to friends to family, fall prey to addiction and have their lives extinguished prematurely. So the fear that this would happen to my child was always present, even as I prayed, desperately prayed, for God to change his trajectory. Navigating the possibility of losing a child while simultaneously clinging to hope for their recovery is excruciating. Period.

It's not easy to hold those two things in tension in your heart: the reality of what your child's lifestyle might lead to, and the truth

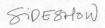

that if he would accept help or believe more in himself and the possibilities of his life, things could be different. To hold on to hope while grappling with what feels inevitable is a tightrope walk. It requires confronting the painful truth of a child's circumstances while fervently believing in the possibility of redemption. No parent wants to say those things to their family members. No parent wants to plan the funeral of their child, even if it's only in our minds, because we know what might happen.

There is an alternate universe I think about often. A place where things are different. It's like those parallel multiverses that comics and DC/Marvel movies capture. In that universe, Brandon is still here and thriving. His laughter still echoes in the halls of our home. He's surpassing me as one of the most successful comedians out there. He has a wonderful family, and he's taking care of his daughter. They are so close. In this alternate universe, we have reconciled. We have forgiven each other. Fully and completely. In the multiverse, when I look into Brandon's eyes, I see nothing but clarity, intention, and ambition. I see him alive.

This is not to say that there are only two ways to be. It isn't addiction and death on one hand and thriving and success on the other. Obviously, there are many points along that spectrum where people are living, surviving, and doing their absolute best. I'd take any of those too. As long as it means that Brandon is here and there's another day and another chance at getting it right.

But I don't live in that alternate universe, do I? And neither do you. We are tethered to this world, to the harsh truths that define our existence. We live in the hard reality that no matter how much we want things to be different, no matter how much we want change or wish we'd said something different or that they'd made a different choice, none of that is what happened. For a parent, the work of grieving is accepting the multiverse is not real. The alternative is not possible—at least not in this life.

The apple doesn't fall far from the tree, they say. The same rebellion that showed up in my dad became the shadows I saw later in my own son. Like me, Brandon inherited my dad's sense of humor. He could crack jokes with the best of them and had begun to really break out in Birmingham as a comedian. But where we differed is that he also took on Dad's rebellious spirit. From his teen years to the last time we spoke two years before he passed away, I always felt him pushing against me. If I told him to go left, he'd go right. If I said the sky was blue, he'd insist it was red. He was like that with everybody. I used to watch him get into arguments with people on social media for no other reason except he wanted to be contrary.

Even during the height of the COVID-19 pandemic, he was pushing back. I asked my children to get vaccinated as soon as the vaccines became available. I'd done my research. I believed the benefits were greater than the risks. But Brandon started undermining me with the younger kids. Sure, he was grown. Nearly thirty at the time. He was able to make a choice for himself. But I didn't appreciate him trying to influence his siblings on something that was life

or death at the time. He would tell them "You don't have to do it"—
and not because he'd done some extensive research and was able to
make a case for why not, but because he was, once again, determined to do the exact opposite of what I said. So whenever they'd
come to me with, "Well, Brandon said . . ." my response was always,
"Did Brandon pay for basketball? Does Brandon pay tuition?" Of
course I was met with silence. "Oh, okay. Go get vaccinated then."

It was never the addiction that drove a wedge between us,
though. I'd gone through this same battle with other members
of our family. My nephew Ron lived with me for a time, and as
I've shared, he, too, ended up passing away from an overdose.
But Ron never disrespected me. And it was the blatant disrespect
I endured from Brandon that created the distance. When he was
younger, I took tough measures with him. The first time I found
drug paraphernalia—bongs and whatnot—in his room, I gathered
them up and lined them along the kitchen counter. Then I just sat in
the living room and waited for him to get home from high school.
When he walked in and saw that I'd found his stash, I'm pretty sure
his heart dropped to the floor. But I didn't say one word and he
didn't come into the living room at first. When he finally did, the
look on his face told me everything I needed to know. That's when
I gathered two of my uncles and we all sat down with him to have a
hard conversation. He apologized for it but apparently didn't stop.

The next time, I found beer and weed in his room. He was in
twelfth grade. This time, I simply said, "I need you to go get your
car detailed." He was so excited. Then I called my niece, who was
two years older than him and a student at Clark Atlanta University.
I told her to come over to the house but get somebody to drop her

off. When Brandon brought the car back gleaming, I handed her the keys and said, "There. You got a car. Have a nice day." I gave his car away right in front of him as a consequence for continuing to drink and smoke. Of course he was beyond mad about that because now he had to ride the cheese wagon (bus) to school like a little kid. From that day on, though, he knew I wasn't playing with him. If he wanted to say and do things that were disrespectful, then he certainly wasn't going to do it while I continued to give him every single privilege and head start I could think of.

That tough love didn't work, though. Just like his grandfather, Brandon defied the warnings. He seemed to have this desperate need to swim upstream when everyone else was going downstream. I never understood it. I know there are seasons in a child's life when they must do their own thing and make their own way, but this felt extreme to me. Despite being taken to church, told right from wrong, and given every privilege I could afford, he still would not listen. To this day, I do not understand it, and part of the grief I hold is that I couldn't figure it out in time. It was something that haunted our relationship until the very end.

In the midst of the pain that followed Brandon's death, there have been moments of light. Moments when I realize that there were some good things being passed down too. My son Malik, who has dealt with anxiety and suicidal thoughts himself, found his strength in going to therapy. He is managing to rise above the shadows and recently graduated from college. In fact, in the months after Brandon died, there were so many times when I found myself slipping into the darkness of grief. But then I'd say, "If I can just get to see my baby boy graduate, then I know I will be okay. Everything will be all right." Well, on December 4, 2023, I watched Malik walk across the stage to accept his degree. I thought my chest would crack open. There was that joy and pain again—living simultaneously in my body, as always. Maybe Malik will be the one to break the chains. I hope so.

It's not lost on me that there's a thread of alternating rebellion and resistance that weaves through three generations. My dad, the suave, funny man fighting his demons the best he knew how but getting caught in the web of addiction, out of the reach of family and friends. Me, on the other end of the line, an abstainer, resisting any connection to drugs and alcohol. And Brandon, whose own rebellious nature returned our line back to addiction, although he fought those demons the best he could.

But as I've said before, I don't know a lot about the hereditary nature of substance abuse. I know it exists. I know there are studies that show that "addiction tends to run in families, and certain types of genes have been linked to different forms of addiction . . . [even though] not all members of an affected family are necessarily prone to addiction."[1] But I can't say if that's what happened in my family. Was it simply a function of the environment both my dad and Brandon chose to be in? Or was it really something that was passed down, a replaying of generational trauma?

If it was the latter, then I can't help but wonder why it skipped me. I'm human. I do not have any special, superhuman ability to resist the temptation of drugs and alcohol. But maybe that thread of rebellion and addiction shows up in other areas of my life, in areas I've yet to unpack. Regardless, I'm still here. They are not. And the pain of realizing that the trauma, whatever its source, did not stop with me can sometimes be hard to bear.

But we aren't in control of any of it, are we? We don't get a say in who ends up with the trait of addiction and who doesn't. And that's the hard part, isn't it? I know what it's like not to be able to put your finger on why this terrible thing has happened to your loved one. But if you are wrestling with this kind of grief, the only thing I can tell you is to keep praying. Keep praying for guidance for yourself and healing for your loved one. Execute every single option you have to help them. If it's drug addiction specifically, keep Narcan in your home in the event there is an overdose and immediate treatment is needed. Take the steps you can. And then, let it go. Surrender any and all outcomes to God.

7

ESTRANGEMENT

To let go does not mean to get rid
of. To let go means to let be.
—JACK KORNFIELD

PARENTING IS A DELICATE DANCE. THERE ARE HIGHS
and lows. Laughter and tears. Pride and disappointment. As they
say, there is no manual. No book that outlines how to raise the
perfect child. When you lay down with someone, you know there's
always a possibility that another life could come from that moment.
But I don't think we always think about all the complexities that
come with raising a human being. As a Black father, I knew the
odds were stacked against us from the start. There is no amount of
preparation or advice that can fully arm you with what you need to
raise a Black boy. Brandon and I were living in a world that tended
to see us as less than worthy, so out the gate, my work as a father

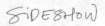

was ten times harder. But I was determined to defy the statistics, to give my son—and all of my children—every opportunity to thrive.

From the moment Brandon came into this world, I was filled with a mix of emotions—joy, apprehension, and an overwhelming sense of responsibility. Of course, I look back and wonder if I could have found a way to bridge the gap between us before it was too late. But deep down, I know the truth. I did the best I could with the tools I had at my disposal. I did what I knew to do. To love him, yes, but also to set boundaries, establish rules, and enforce consequences. Yet, in those later years, we simply clashed, argued, and drifted apart. It was a continuous cycle of anger, frustration, and resentment.

The two years Brandon and I went without speaking were extremely tough. All our communication was filtered through my mother or his lawyer. The lawyer was because I was still trying to help him resolve the legal trouble he'd gotten into over the years. I didn't necessarily *want* us to stop speaking. I didn't separate myself from him without considerable thought. But the ups and downs of our relationship had taken their toll, and I found myself at a point where I needed to protect my peace. I was very familiar with what drug abuse can do to families. This wasn't my first rodeo. Addiction can breed toxicity and end up causing pain and stress for the loved ones who are only trying to help. Honestly, dealing with all the back-and-forth with Brandon was a distraction and a drain. Despite having two children I was putting through college, Aaryn and Malik, most of my resources were going to Brandon, and he was the adult. I had other children, grandkids, and godchildren to consider in all this. I had to draw the line.

The disrespect I faced was completely unreal. There were so many times when Brandon, driven by his need, would do and say things I just could not stomach. You can't talk to a Black dad just any ol' kind of way. I wasn't just a visitation dad. I had custody of him since he was fourteen years old. I raised him, sent him off to college, and bought him what he needed and more of what he wanted. I wasn't just going to let stuff fly. Sometimes he'd say things that made me want to hop in my car (like my granddaddy did with my own father when he found out his son had pushed my grandmother) and settle things with my child right then and there. But I didn't. I kept supporting him. Kept trying to get him help. Kept trying to talk to him. Kept praying for him. I'd given him my all. And still, nothing changed.

I had to let him go.

When Brandon passed away, there were so many people, family members even, who implied that I should feel guilty because we weren't speaking when he died. They are wrong. How was I to know when he was going to die? Life is too short to hold something as heavy as guilt. Honestly, in the same two years we didn't speak, with the amount of stress I was under, I could have died. How would my death have affected him? Would people be asking him if he felt guilty? And what about my other children who aren't perfect but were doing their best? Did they not deserve to have a father who was well? It's all too much. The hard, hard truth is, when you cut people off, you risk losing them before you can reconcile. That is the chance you take. That was the chance I took.

Whenever you decide to sever ties with someone, there's a risk of irreparable fallout. This is especially true with loved ones—family and friends whose toxic behavior necessitates the break. You might also, from a distance, have to watch their toxic behavior change their lives for the worse or take them out altogether. It's agonizing. Nobody wants that. But it still doesn't change the necessity of separating from people who cannot stop causing you hardship and pain. Yes, I firmly believe our job as parents, as people, is to serve and love the best we can, but we must try to do that from a full cup. If the same people we are trying to help are draining us, we are essentially causing problems for our own mental health, to the extent that we can't be the help we want to be for them. We must be able to prioritize our well-being by disengaging from those causing us distress, even if they're dear to us. While our duty is to support and love, it's futile to do so from an empty reservoir.

When we're in the vicious cycle of trying to help someone who doesn't want to be helped, someone who might be acting out and behaving in toxic ways, it will likely cause pain and undue trauma for ourselves. And then we can't do what we need to do. Trying to assist the unyielding only perpetuates our own misery. So once again, we are back to one of the biggest themes of our grief journeys— acceptance. We must accept the fact that when we detach, when we create distance, whether temporarily or permanently, we could lose them altogether. I would like to say that the pain of not distancing has to be greater than the pain of loss—that the agony of maintaining the status quo in relationships must outweigh the potential sorrow of separation. But that doesn't feel right. Not now, at least. Because the pain of losing my son has been greater than any pain I can ever imagine.

I didn't know what was coming down the line. And I don't know now what horrors might have happened for me or my children had I kept him close. How was I supposed to know what to do? It's a hard dilemma for anyone, but especially parents who tend to cling to the belief that love conquers all. You want to believe that your love is deeper and greater than anything this person to whom you gave birth could do to you. As Scripture says, love covers a multitude of sins (1 Peter 4:8). But at some point, separating yourself from the thing that's causing you pain so that you can heal from that pain has to be part of the equation. It has to be a possibility available to you. While love may indeed conquer all in the end, it doesn't negate the importance of setting boundaries and prioritizing personal healing.

There's no gentle way to distance oneself, especially from a child. No manual for detachment. There's no happy way to go about letting a child go. It will never feel good. And yet, if you're pushed to the edge of your sanity, it makes sense to do it anyway, with the full knowledge that doing so could mean that the last time you see a person on this earth will be the moment you made the decision to part from them. Whew! That's hard. And real deep. And not something people think about as they flippantly talk about cutting folks off. Social media platforms are rife with memes advocating for self-preservation and detachment without fully comprehending the ramifications. People will cosign these acts of cutting off dead weight, or letting people go, without really knowing the consequences or being able to accept what that might really mean. I, more than anybody, know now what that really means.

Do I regret that Brandon and I didn't get a chance to meet up that week like we were planning to? Yes, of course. We were scheduled to meet just days after he died, and I think often about what that conversation might have been like, how I might have at least been able to say, "I love you" one more time. Do I regret that he lost his life before we could sit down and hash things out? Absolutely. Fate has a cruel sense of timing sometimes. I think about whether I should have sent him to rehab one more time. Maybe the third time really would have been the charm. But guilt? I don't feel that. I feel no guilt about stepping away when my own mental health required me to.

If Brandon were to come back from the grave, my boundaries would remain the same. I am not diverting from my parenting principles to make anybody feel comfortable or to give anybody the excuse or reason they need for why this may have happened. There was no excuse for Brandon to die. He made bad choices when he was told not to. He was raised right. He was taken to church. I cooked for him. Washed his clothes. Hugged and kissed him. When it was thundering and lightning, he slept in my bed when he was little. He curled up under me so he'd feel safe from the storm. A lack of love could never be the reason.

How was I supposed to know he'd be gone so soon? Life doesn't come with a crystal ball, and guilt trips don't change the decisions we've already made. I always held out hope for change. But when it didn't look like change was going to happen, I think the distance might have helped my heart survive the news.

Miss Jannie, a longtime family friend who helped me raise my kids, called me a couple of months before Brandon passed and said, "They're baptizing Brandon today. You need to come up here."

I told her no.

Why? Well, honestly, I didn't want to come to the baptismal service and go through all that emotional upheaval without having practical resolutions to the breach in our relationship. I wanted to sit down and have a conversation with my son before we did anything that would suck me back into the vortex that was his life. I was stuck on that. And yes, when I think about it now, a part of me wishes I had gone. But there's another part of me that is glad I didn't. I think the anguish I would have felt when he passed would've been worse had I gone. Maybe God gave me that space, because if I had seen him get baptized, if I had celebrated that monumental step he took in his spiritual life, I think the pain I would have felt when I got that devastating call would have taken me out of here. I would not have survived it.

Brandon had been dishonest too often. So the consequence of that dishonesty was that he was losing the people around him. Even though I wasn't in communication with him, I was still working behind the scenes to help him. When he was struggling with being able to see his baby, my granddaughter, I intervened in hopes that maybe there could be some supervised visits. But it didn't work out. So I went down to the courthouse and paid attorney fees so he could fight for his child in court. He sent a message to me through his lawyer that day: "Tell Dad I said thank you."

When she called me and told me what he said, I responded in kind: "Tell him I said he's welcome."

That's it. It was the way it had to be. All because Brandon was still using, and I knew it.

So no, I do not feel guilty. Any parent will tell you—especially those who have lost children—there are no easy answers when it

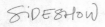

comes to raising a child. Each decision is filled with uncertainty. But we press on, driven by love, guided by faith, and fueled by the hope that we're doing the right thing. I knew the risks when I made the decision to stop speaking to my son. As I shared, I'd already prepared my other kids for what might come. I've never been one to sugarcoat reality to them or anyone else. I knew what Brandon was into, and I knew the dangers. When I saw the signs, heard the whispers, I prepared for the worst. Fentanyl is a deadly game nobody should be playing.

The last time I saw Brandon alive was at my uncle Herbert's funeral, which happened to be the same week as my nephew Ron's, who also passed of an overdose. Brandon walked in and sat two rows in front of me. We didn't speak much that day, but I look back now and see just how much of a warning Ron's death was for Brandon. It was a grim reminder of how fragile life truly is, a reminder he didn't pay attention to. As a result, he ended up in the same place Ron did. In a way, I think God was showing me at Uncle Herbert's funeral that Brandon was either going to go left or right, but the decision of which way to go would be solely his.

Brandon was my firstborn, my pride and joy. He used to joke with his siblings that he had a better childhood than they did because I was younger when he was born. "I had the best because Dad is old now. He be taking naps all the time. Ain't got no energy. Back in the day, though, we went everywhere." I can't help but wonder—maybe I did too much? Maybe all the ways I provided for and included him turned out to be too much. For years he rode shotgun with me, just the two of us against the world. But even with all that love and attention, it wasn't enough to save him from himself. A half million dollars of rehab and legal fees later, all I ended up with was a casket and no more years with my son. Even thinking about that now makes me just as angry as it does sad. But I suppose it is what it is. I loved Brandon. I gave him what I thought he needed. And he made his choice.

The rawness of all this feels like it won't go away. There are no nice, neat endings to this part of the story. I was and am consumed by grief, overwhelmed by a sense of loss that feels like it can swallow me whole on my worst days. In the midst of our estrangement, I had been clinging to the hope that one day we would find our way back to each other. I held on to the belief that time could heal even the deepest wounds. But it doesn't always happen like that. And sometimes we have to accept that we can give our kids everything and their lives still do not turn out the way we hoped.

That same grief has also hit our family—his siblings especially—hard. I will say it over and over again: We loved Brandon so much. And it's hard to realize that our love might not have been enough. Yes, he had our love. Yes, he even had fans because of the reality show he was on and his burgeoning comedy career. Yes, he had every resource at his disposal, every opportunity to turn things around. But again, he made his choices. So none of those things mattered in the end. None of it was enough. And now we're left picking up the pieces. We are left with nowhere to put that love. Man, that's a tough pill to swallow.

8

GRIEF TIMES FOUR

Children are often the forgotten grievers.
—DAVID KESSLER

"YOU STRAIGHT, DAD?" MALIK ASKED AS HE WAS ABOUT to leave the house.

"I'm good," I responded.

I could hear it in his voice. He was concerned. Even though I couldn't really release all my tears yet, I know Malik felt me. He felt the pain I was going through that day. It was the first few days after Brandon's passing, and everyone had finally left the house. Nobody was there but me and Malik. I was sitting in the chair by the fireplace with my legs crossed when he leaned over and hugged me three or four times. Then he checked in again to see if I was okay.

"I'm okay, Malik."

I could tell he didn't want to leave. He was afraid. As perceptive

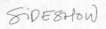

as we can be as parents, our children are just as or even more perceptive when it comes to us. They feel us. They discern what's going on even if they don't always have the words to explain it. Malik was sensing that I was holding back. He also knew I would never break down in front of him.

But between me and you, I'm still hoping that I told him the truth. That I will be okay one day. That's the work for me. I'm healing, not healed. It's an ongoing thing. But above and beyond dealing with my own grief over this last year, one of the hardest things I've had to do was help my children navigate their sorrow. Because each of them—D'essence, Malik, and Aaryn—are so different, it's like walking through a minefield of emotions most days. Each step means the possibility of triggering another explosion of tears and heartache.

On this day in particular, though, I was trying to gauge Malik's emotions just as much as he was trying to gauge mine. I could feel a kind of clinging beneath the warmth of his embrace. Whenever I tried to pull out of the hug, he'd hold tighter, refusing to let me go. I wanted to reassure him. I wanted to ease the burden of worry. But I couldn't lie to him either. This thing was heavy. It had shaken us all to the core. Brandon's death had created a gaping hole in our souls, and it took everything we had not to be taken out by it all.

So for Malik, I devised little rituals to reassure him. These were small acts of comfort to soothe any anxiety he might have been feeling and ease any pain from the loss. I'd do small things to distract him from the empty chair by the fireplace where Brandon used to sit. I made sure he saw me moving around. Whenever he was about to leave for school after a visit, I made sure to walk him to his truck, pretending to inspect tires or check the back seat. I still do this even a year later because I know there is no timeline for grief.

I've also driven seventy miles to Montgomery to have lunch with him or hang out in his apartment just so he could see my face and I could see his. I want him to know that I'm here for him, and that while I acknowledge his sorrow, I also will, if I can, try to shield him and his sisters from the full weight and impact of it.

But listen: grief don't care nothing about what I'm trying to do. That's the funny part. Or maybe the not-so-funny part, if I think hard enough about it. Grief doesn't follow any script and doesn't play fair. Them waves will come out of nowhere and smack you around when you least expect it. I've found myself laughing and joking with my morning show family, and some small thing will happen—maybe it's a song I hear or a word someone says—and before I know it, I'm laid out. So as much as I try to take some of the burden of my children's pain, I also know my kids will have to deal with it in their own way. Their grief has manifested—continues to manifest—in different ways.

For the most part, Aaryn and Malik both channeled their pain into their studies. They threw themselves into their schoolwork until it was borderline obsessive. Malik also dove even further into sports. He went to work for the college basketball team, and that kept him busy. I guess this was their way of coping and maybe finding some purpose in it all. Brandon loved them and wanted them to do well, so it seemed like they used that knowledge to drive them to do just that. Out of the two, though, I believe Aaryn is the one who has had to work through compounded trauma with the loss of her brother. During the Fourth of July weekend in 2020, Aaryn was shot as an innocent bystander at a stoplight in Houston—a nightmare that played out in headlines and blog posts the entire week. She and her boyfriend were making a run to Whataburger when a car pulled up on the other side of the car next to them. A shootout took place and Aaryn was caught in the crossfire, taking a bullet to her leg. Because of that she was thrust into a whirlwind of panic and PTSD (post-traumatic stress disorder) that I'm sure was only amplified when she found out Brandon died. Yet, somehow, in the midst of the chaos and revisited trauma, and with the help of therapy and late-night conversations with me, both Aaryn and Malik are finding their footing.

My oldest daughter, D'essence, is a different story. Stubborn as a mule and twice as fierce, she has struggled. Even before Brandon passed, she had already begun making some really bad decisions. So much so that our relationship seemed to be going the same route mine did with Brandon. The idea that I might have to distance myself from her was so hard to process, especially since she'd just had my grandbaby. But just like with Brandon, there's only so much disrespect I can take, and I always feel like it's better for me to cut off communication than to continue to go back and forth and make things worse.

After Brandon died, D'essence started to act out more. She resisted every attempt I made to help her and often retreated into herself. Whenever I heard or saw some of the things she was doing, alarm bells would ring in my head. It was like watching a rerun of my son's mistakes, a painful reminder of the dangers that can come when emotional pain isn't addressed. There was even one point, around nine months after we lost Brandon, when D'essence just disappeared. Her mother called me crying because no one knew where she was. Apparently, a friend of hers in Atlanta was answering her phone. The girl was drunk and crying, saying that she and D'essence were in a nightclub and, leaving her purse and credit cards behind, my daughter just vanished. My heart was broken. *I just know God isn't putting me through this again*, I thought. To help find her, I hired a private investigator to track her down, and eventually she came back home. That's when I sent her to a therapeutic facility that was supposed to help her deal with whatever had caused her to just up and leave like that.

After she returned from the facility, D'essence wrote me and her mother a letter doing her version of "setting boundaries." In my mind at the time, it sounded a lot like "I don't need you to be my father anymore," and that hurt like hell. If I'm honest, I didn't know how to process what she was saying. D'essence isn't my biological daughter, but I'd raised her for most of her life. She is Malik's older sister, and I was in a relationship with their mother for a very long time. I don't know how to be anything else but her father. So my question to her was, "If I'm not serving in that capacity for you, then what do we have exactly?" Her answer became quite clear. For a while, we didn't have anything. Which, as I said, hurt something terrible. But I now know that grief manifests in all kinds of ways. People deal with those crazy waves the best way they know how, and this was hers.

Despite it all, there eventually came a glint of light shining through the darkness of that time with my oldest daughter. We slowly but surely came around to each other. I can't help but admire D'essence's resilience. Even as she tries to figure out her life, especially dealing with the pressures of being a new mom, I can now see that she's trying hard not to be defined by her pain. In this new role as the oldest child, she's had to hold so much sorrow—from dealing with Brandon's death to all the unexpected twists that came afterward. Of course it's hard. Some people deal with grief by pushing forward, and some people shut down. You never know which one you're going to be until you're acting it out. But she is figuring it out. We all are.

For me, I try to find balance any way I can. I need those times when I can laugh just as much as I need space to cry. I tell my kids all the time that this is how we will all stay strong as we hold so much sorrow. Yes, we grieve. Yes, we get therapy and have our moments. But we survive. We don't give up. I could have taken myself out, the pain was that bad. There were times when I seriously thought about it. But God held me together. There's no other way to explain it. God blocked it.

Helping children navigate grief is heavy. As a parent, I carry not just my own pain but the pain of my children. Children who don't have the lived experience to know how to deal with the pain of loss. After living over five decades on this earth, I have seen some things. I've experienced the impact of death multiple times over, including the death of family members. What it feels like and how it changes you. I don't think there is any death that can compare to the loss of a child. That is an entirely different category of loss and grief. It's an anguish I don't wish on my worst enemy. But I've still lived long enough to have experienced grief and loss in a way that my children have not. And so, guiding them through their very early understandings of grief and loss is beyond painful. Because at what point do you hold back your tears to let your child cry? At what point do you teach your child how to still get up and go to school or work every day, how to still get up and take care of their own children, even as their hearts are broken?

Some parents simply don't do it. I think I understand why. We hear stories all the time about children who say, "Well, when my father died, nobody took care of me." Or "When my mother passed away, no one paid attention to how it impacted me." I've witnessed firsthand the struggles of my mother and grandparents as they managed their own grief. I watched how they dealt with the death of my father, while I wondered why no one came to see about me. But I know now that it wasn't a matter of unwillingness but rather an acknowledgment of their limited capacity. This way of letting children fend for themselves is not a function of parents not *wanting* to help their child grieve. It's likely they just don't know how to. They may want to reach out and be there, but if they aren't even navigating their own grief well—whatever that means—then they are likely feeling completely incapable of helping their child with the same grief.

There are things I wanted to say to Malik and D'essence. Things I wanted to talk to Aaryn about. But I just couldn't. There were many times when I knew I was about to break, but I set my emotions aside because I saw in their faces that they needed something different from me in the moment. And I don't know if that was good or healthy for me, but it's something I did because I didn't want them feeling even a portion of what I was feeling.

In this grief, I don't always know what to say. I don't always know what to do. There are always questions. Am I doing enough? Are my actions lining up with what my children need? I may not always have the answers, but I refuse to let fear or uncertainty dictate my actions. And I think maybe that's the point. Maybe part of what this grieving journey teaches us is that we are not always going to know what to do and what to say. Being a parent reveals to us very early on that we don't know what to do or say all the time anyway. Yet we wake up every day trying to do our best. So maybe we need a kind of surrender. When we are helping our children grieve, we just have to try to do our best and let God do the rest.

We won't do it perfectly. If we don't parent perfectly on a good day, when everything is sparkling and new and wonderful, we surely are not going to parent perfectly when things are hard and our children are hurting. So choose grace. That's what I've had to do. There are times when I might have been too harsh with my words out of fear or pain. Too quick to jump to a conclusion or not quick enough. But I've chosen not to judge what I could have done or said in the aftermath of Brandon's death, nor judge what my children could have or should have done or said. I simply wake up every day with a renewed intention of trying to help them through their pain however it shows up. In the midst of whatever doubt might be present, I promise to show up, do my best, and offer my children the love and support they need.

It's more than what we do or say that helps them grieve. How *we* grieve, how *we* model the grieving process for them will be the greatest help to them, even if we never say "the right thing" to them about their pain or their loss. Our actions are what make the deepest impression on those we love.

I know my children are watching me. I know they're wanting to see from me if it's okay to cry, if it's okay to scream, if it's okay to pray or mourn. And so I want them to see that, yes, it is okay. More than me being there for them, talking to them on the phone, and guiding them, I want to model for them what a good griever looks like, what a mourner looks like. Someone who is still showing up to life every day but is not afraid to say, "I miss my son, and I am hurting and in pain." That's what I want to give to them. And so I wake up every day trying to do exactly that.

My children are proof that resilience runs deep and wide throughout our family. God has kept us all in ways I never could have expected. Yes, therapy has been our lifeline. And sharing my grief journey with friends, followers, and fans has helped me tremendously. I don't know if I can fully explain it, but there's something about pouring my heart out to strangers. People who I know have gone through similar or worse. It makes me feel like I'm not alone. That we are not alone. And yet, I also know that if I did not have the platform I do or the people to talk to, God would still be here, holding me together. Giving me the words to say to my babies when they need them. Keeping my anger from overtaking me. Helping me to use laughter to sustain us.

Solomon got it right in Ecclesiastes 3:1–4:

For everything there is a season, and a time for every matter under heaven: a time to be born, and a time to die; a time to plant, and a

time to pluck up what is planted; a time to kill, and a time to heal;
a time to break down, and a time to build up; a time to weep, and
a time to laugh; a time to mourn, and a time to dance.

This is a core lesson I've learned throughout this experience.
One I hope my children are learning: Many things can be true. We
can be happy and sad. We can be ready to take on the world one day
and ready to go to bed forever the next. Grief is part of the human
experience. Sorrow is as necessary as love and joy. So we don't have
to be afraid when grief shows up. We can cry when we need to and
laugh when we need to. It's all part of the cycle of life. Even though
this has been a painful season for us, I believe that God will allow
the pendulum to swing the other way. Eventually.

9

BURYING MY BABY BOY

Say not in grief that he is no more but
live in thankfulness that he was.
—HEBREW PROVERB

THE WEEK I BURIED BRANDON IT FELT LIKE I WAS WALK-
ing around in a perpetual rainstorm. Dark clouds hung heavy over
me, and it truly took a wide range of support to help me get through
it all. One of the people who really stood in the gap for me was my
pastor in Alabama, Reverend John King. He came to me in my darkest hour because he understood exactly what I was going through.
He'd lost his own son to an overdose and had walked this same road
only a few years before me. I remember being distraught one day,
crying on the phone with him, and the first thing I noticed was that
he didn't judge me. He didn't tell me to hold it together, even though
that's what I'd been trying to do. He just preached life back into my

body. He gave me so much amazing perspective about the stage of the grief process I was in, and his words, soaked with empathy and wisdom, offered me a lifeline of hope in the middle of my grief.

Then, believe it or not, President Joe Biden also offered a bit of light during this time. His personal letter to me acknowledging my pain and speaking my son's name meant everything. He shared with me how he felt when his own son Beau passed away and gave me so many words of hope and encouragement. I couldn't help but to feel blessed that here was our country's head of state taking the time to reach out and share his sympathies with me. Along with that letter, my spirit was buoyed by the calls I received from Vice President Kamala Harris. She's a member of Alpha Kappa Alpha Sorority, Inc., part of the Divine Nine of Historically Black Fraternities and Sororities that I'm a part of, so there was an immediate connection. When we talked, she spoke to me like a fellow Greek, and that familiarity was what I needed. It grounded me.

That Wednesday after Brandon passed, as I was planning the funeral, I went back to work. I returned to the radio. It was hard but necessary. I needed the safety of that space. My job is essentially spending my mornings bringing laughter and music to listeners' lives, so I knew doing that in the middle of my own tragedy could provide me a kind of refuge. Again, it was not easy. Especially that first week. And even now, it can be hard to listen to a song on our playlist and not break down. Some of the music we play overwhelms me, leaving me vulnerable and raw. That first week, though, "Free Mind" by Tems laid me out. It was a favorite of Brandon's, and I saw his face when it played.

Perhaps the hardest part about going back into "the office" was seeing the faces of those I worked with who also loved Brandon. The colleagues and friends who tried to save my son. When I shook my cohost Special K's hand, I felt sad. And maybe a little embarrassed. He was one of the ones who was truly trying to get Brandon the help he needed. He'd been talking to him quite a bit and had worked with Brenda to get him to go to a rehab out in Phoenix. Unfortunately, Brandon signed himself out of the facility before getting all the way free. So seeing Special K with tears in his eyes just wiped me out. He was like an uncle to my boy.

Then there's Da Brat, who was sitting at the studio desk with shades on when I walked in that day. I couldn't even make eye contact with her because our relationship was deep and personal. She knows me, having been raised by her grandparents as well. Our connection is so real, and I could see the pain on her face. She had been trying to help Brandon too.

Seeing the tears in their eyes, feeling their sorrow, was a reminder that this loss of mine reverberated beyond my family. So when Tems, with her soulful voice and Nigerian lilt, sang "I try to be fine but I can't be,"[1] I determined to allow myself to feel everything. Even the hard stuff. By still going into work every day, I learned to give myself grace, step away if I need to, and take the time I need to collect myself before returning to the mic.

I was blessed to have so many people reach out to me after hearing about Brandon's passing. But I have to admit that there's something about standing in the funeral home, looking at your baby in a casket, that takes you to another place. You feel so hurt, so heartbroken, so helpless in that moment. No amount of "I'm sorrys" or "My condolences" can change what that feels like. Before they transported my boy from the morgue to the viewing area, I remember standing there looking at him and thinking about ways I could still show him I love him. Even then, with dimensions between us. The only thing I could think of was getting his favorite bottle of cologne, Bond No. 9, from Neiman Marcus, and spraying him with it. I don't know why I did it. There is a kind of sterile scent in a funeral home, but it wasn't just about that. It just felt right. Like the times I helped him tie his shoe when he was little or tie a tie when he went to a dance, this was my final act of love as his father.

It was so cloudy and rainy the day of the funeral. And I know if I google it, there are probably a million and one people sharing what rain on the day of a funeral means. But I don't care. Because on the limousine ride over, even as I was thinking about how Brenda, Brandon's mother; Taurus, his stepfather; and my children and mother were feeling, I got my own answer. As we were driving down the road, I looked out the window and saw a break in the clouds. Through the break came a ray of sunshine. To me, it felt like the heavens were offering solace. It was like God was saying, *I'm here. I have your baby boy. He's good now.* Seeing that little sliver of light helped me to see the light that showed up in other ways that day.

In the planning and preparation for the funeral, I wanted to make sure every detail was meticulously attended to. I didn't want Brenda to do a single thing. If I was hurting, I knew she was torn up inside. This was her first baby. The one she carried in her body for nine months. I didn't want to add to her pain or burden her in any way. Before she arrived for the viewing, I realized they had put the wrong shirt on Brandon. We'd selected a black button-down and they'd put on a white one. So when they began rolling to the back to fix it, I saw the look in Brenda's eyes and knew she was about to go to the back with them and change the shirt herself. But there ain't no way I could let that happen. And I didn't. The staff ended up changing the shirt, and I oversaw everything. It was the hardest thing I did that day.

I think that was the moment when the fact that Brandon was gone really crystalized in my mind. When I saw them changing his shirt and I could see that his body had no life in it, well, that was truly a living nightmare. I wanted to scream. I didn't, but I wanted to. Still, if I had to endure that image in order to prevent his mother from doing so, then that's what I had to do. It was important to me that what *I* saw would not be the last image his mother had of him.

So I did it. I watched them carefully hold the unyielding body of my boy as they changed his shirt. Because that's what dads do. And no matter what, I was going to be a dad to Brandon until the very end. I believe that dads see things through. They make sure everything is right. I needed to make sure everything was right for Brandon. I needed him to see that I was right there. Even before that moment with the shirt, when they brought him in from the morgue, I watched as they put him on the table. I watched and I didn't blink. I didn't faint. I didn't pass out. I just did what needed to be done.

From selecting his final resting place to choosing the suit he wore, I took care of it all. As hard as it was, that week I told grief to square up. I would eventually crumble, yes. Every emotion burst forth at the cemetery when they finally lowered Brandon into the ground. But before that, I did what my granddaddy taught me. I became the rock for my family to lean on. Because that's what fathers do, isn't it? Even when the ground beneath us threatens to

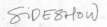

swallow us. Even when anger is simmering underneath our skin and we are screaming on the inside, *Why did he have to die?* We stand firm.

From that moment on, it was nothing but back-to-back moments of unexpected grace. The funeral service was held at noon on Saturday, February 4, at Faith Chapel in Birmingham. That morning, I'd gone back to the funeral home because Brenda told me she wanted to see him one more time before they moved him to the church. When we arrived, Craig and Journey, friends of our family who were raised with Brandon, were there, distraught because they missed the viewing and didn't get a chance to see him before the staff closed and locked the casket for transport. Thankfully, Ms. Rachel, the funeral director, saw how upset they were and handed me the key to the casket—something that is rarely done. It felt like a gesture of trust that, to this day, I do not take for granted.

"Just unlock the bottom and it will open," she said.

After opening the casket, I let Craig and Journey see Brandon, and when I tell you they tore that whole chapel up? I mean, they cried and cried and cried. At about 10:15 a.m., the staff started coming in to gather the flowers and casket for transport. Ms. Rachel sensed that we were having a moment and quietly said, "We're going to head over to the church."

"Yes, ma'am," I said.

"Okay, I'll give you a few more minutes," she continued.

"Yes, ma'am."

She paused and looked at us for a minute. Then she said, "Y'all want to close him up and roll him out to the car?"

"Yes, ma'am."

And that was that. We rolled the casket out to the Suburban that waited at the end of the walkway. Brandon and I had an ongoing joke that if either one of us died, we didn't want to be put in a hearse. We both thought they were creepy as hell. So to honor that, I chose a big-bodied truck that felt like something he would have wanted.

When we got to the SUV, Brandon's friends and I said our final goodbyes. I leaned over and kissed my boy on the forehead, and we all lowered the casket down into the space, closing the doors behind it. Then I turned around and walked back into the funeral home where a barber was waiting to cut my hair before the church service.

After changing my clothes, I drove myself over to the church to make sure everything was set up right before the start of the service. Then I met my family in the parking lot where we lined up to enter. I looked around at my family. I saw Brandon's mother and stepfather, my mother and children, aunts and uncles and close family friends. I couldn't help but think about how backward this all was. As parents, we bring our children into the world, never imagining that we would have to send them out. But there I was doing exactly that. My mom is seventy-five. When it's her time to go, I will be devastated, but it will make sense because of her age. And then after her, it's me. I'm middle-aged. So I'm next in line to see glory. Then after me, it's supposed to be my kids. *After* me. Something is terribly wrong when your kids go before you. It's out of order. And when stuff is out of order and with no warning, it changes everything.

All that said, there were absolutely points during the funeral and

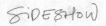

immediately after when the weight was lifted for a little while. When there were more smiles than tears. I'm not going to be able to be anywhere, even my son's homegoing, and there not be laughter. So the times when joy met my pain were much appreciated. Like when I was walking down the aisle toward the casket with my family at the service and I saw Juicy (Shirlene King Pearson), comedian and former star of the reality television show *Little Women: Atlanta*, standing there at the end of a row. I immediately jumped out of line and kissed her on the cheek. "Boy, you so crazy! You need to go get back in line," she said while we both laughed. Or when I watched my granddaughter smiling and mimicking me as I worshipped. That levity helped push me through the harder moments that came as we celebrated Brandon's life.

Later that day, after we all left the cemetery, my uncle Suge started to drive me back to the church to pick up my truck. But after a few minutes, I changed my mind.

"Can you just take me home?" I asked.

When I got to the house, Gale, my friend and personal chef, was there with a delicious layout of food waiting. The fireplace was lit, and all I needed to do was sit, eat, and rest a bit before I had to get back up again and go to the repast. This was great because, in that moment, I was cold, sad, and hungry. So that's what I did. I had a quiet dinner with Uncle Suge; Brandon's first girlfriend, Bianca; and Uncle Suge's daughters, Victoria and Veronica. Then I sat on my couch and rested my mind and heart for a beat.

After a little while, everyone began to head out to the repast. We'd rented a beautiful facility, and it was truly going to be a time of fellowship with the family and friends who loved Brandon.

"I'm going to change clothes before I go over. I need to take this suit off because it's uncomfortable," I said.

They all said okay and left. Not too long after, the doorbell rang. When I opened the door, my grandbaby ran into the room followed by her mother.

"I want to swing, Papa!" she said.

"Okay," I said. "We can go swing. Whatever you want to do."

By then, I had put on my jogging suit and could finally stretch my legs some and relax my body. Exhaustion was tearing me up on the inside. I felt like my whole body had been drained of tears. But when my grandbaby suggested that we go swing on the play-set I have in my backyard, I thought, *Why not?* And more than a repast, that's what I needed. As I pushed her, I could hear the ducks nearby. I saw the geese flying over us. Baby girl kept saying, "Wheeeee!" And I took a deep breath. One I felt like I'd been holding for a week. What a sight we must have been to anyone who knew what was going on. Me, pushing a little girl on a swing who'd just lost her father. A father who'd lost his son, pushing a little girl on a swing.

While I was still outside, the coordinator handling logistics for the repast called me.

"Hey, Rickey! Everybody's here at the repast waiting to greet you. You on your way?"

"I'm not going to be able to make it. I'm pushing my grand-daughter on a swing," I said.

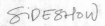

And that's it. It was what it was. What it had to be. "Just tell all my close friends to come by the house," I told the woman. "I'm going to stay with her. I can't leave her side." The repast went on without me.

Me and my grandbaby stayed outside for a good hour and a half. It was cold, and both of our noses were running by the time we were done. None of that mattered, though. I needed to be there with her. She was only three. Of course she didn't know what had happened. How do you even explain to a toddler that her father is dead? So I just decided to be there. And, in her own little way, she was there for me.

In the midst of grief and sorrow and rage, there is gratitude. I am thankful for the moments I shared with Brandon. The memories I will cherish forever. I am also grateful for the ways God has shown up for me through this process. The way He has held me up when I didn't know if I could stand. The way He has given me the strength to carry on. I thank God for the courage and resilience that have come from the loss.

To be clear, though, I'm never "getting over" this. My grandparents never got over the loss of my father. My granddaddy was almost ninety-three when he passed, and I know it still weighed on his heart. You don't get over it, but you do learn to live with it. Despite it feeling like leprosy some days. Like there's something weirdly noticeable about you. Like the loss creates emotional spots and bruises on your person. I'm walking around like a human-sized open sore and, with God's guidance, just figuring out how to deal with it.

In fact, I firmly believe that we don't get over our losses; we just expand to make room for them. Losing a loved one doesn't mean we can never have joy again or that life doesn't keep going. It doesn't mean that peace will forever elude us. What it does mean is that we become bigger in spirit. We have now been required to hold more love. Our love for those we've lost expands us. And yes, having the capacity to hold more love also means we have the capacity to hold more grief. That's the unintended consequence, I guess. But we can also hold more of the other emotions and fruit of the Spirit available to us. Joy, peace, contentment. We just have to make room for it.

I love to hear about the examples of grief that are in the Bible. In biblical days, they took time to mourn. Nearly every account is filled with examples of individuals grappling with profound loss. Some wore specific clothes that symbolized the state they were in. They openly demonstrated the intensity of their grief, like when David stripped off his outer garments because he was so rent with pain and sorrow at the death of King Saul (2 Samuel 1:11–12). Even Jesus, dealing with the weight of the pending cross, prayed and cried out in agony in the garden of Gethsemane with sweat like drops of blood (Luke 22:44).

I hope to see a day when grief is normalized in a way it isn't yet. When it will be okay to see people grieving and allow people to feel all the emotions that come with that grief. Instead, too many people tell those who are grieving when *they* think it's time for them to move on. Or they say things like, "Don't you think it's time to get over it?" Instead of urging others to move on or get over it, we should make room for their feelings.

The truth is, there is no getting over the loss of a child. For the rest of my life, I will feel the pain of Brandon no longer being here. At the same time, I will still laugh and I will still cry. I will still get on the stage and perform my butt off, and come off that stage and maybe cry my eyes out. Some days I might just be still and other days I might dance around the room with my grandbaby. I'm going to grieve and I'm going to also do the things that make a life a life. One of the pieces of this life of mine will always be the grief I carry because Brandon is not here anymore. That's got to be okay too.

This is partly why I talk about him publicly and post about him on social media. I want to destigmatize the experience of grief and create space for honest and open dialogue. I want others to know that it is okay to feel sad, angry, or lost. These are the natural responses to pain. I want people to really understand that grief is part of life. That if you live long enough, you will lose someone you love. We don't have to hide that reality. We don't have to put it away so we don't make people uncomfortable. We don't have to get over it. All we have to do is make room for it in the course of our lives. When we make room for the fact that grief may show up one day and joy and laughter the next day, then it's safe to say we are healing. The more we allow people to feel their feelings, to grieve openly, the less likely the grief will have a negative impact on their lives.

Why do we hide our grief? I've known people who are two and three and four years past the loss of their family member and they still haven't cried about it. They still haven't released anything.

Holding that level of pain is bound to have a physical impact on you. Your body always responds to the ache that's in your heart. We can't continue to allow ourselves to be walking tombs, walking around with all this heaviness inside us, too afraid to show how we're feeling because we think we'll be judged or people will call us weak. This only perpetuates the cycle of silence and shame surrounding grief, making it even harder for those who are struggling to reach out for support.

There's nothing weak about vulnerability. There's nothing weak about sharing your heart and letting people know where you are in any given moment. Yet we still have this stigma, especially in certain communities, where we're taught that we only get to be strong. In the Black community, strength is everything. It's like a high-value currency. If you're strong, then you can get through anything. But I think the people who are the strongest are those who are most vulnerable. The people who know how to release, who know how to put their grief in its proper place, are the ones who are actually the strongest. And those who are pretending not to have any emotions at all, who pretend that grief happens in this finite period of time, are the ones who need the most healing. They're putting in a lot of work to try and make it seem like they don't need anything or anybody, when really, they need everything and everybody.

Part of getting well is allowing ourselves to openly mourn those we love and being unafraid of what that might look like. Once people stop caring about what others say or think about it, the less others will say or think about it. Grieving will become part of everyday life.

"Oh, Rickey is grieving. He is mourning," they will say. And it will be okay.

"Rickey is having a tough time today," they'll say. And that will be okay too.

Christians are often taught that grief is a journey. And it is. I will be grieving Brandon, to varying degrees and in various ways, for the rest of my life. But I also know that in the depths of sorrow, there must be hope. On our dark days, we must believe that the sun will break through the clouds and see it as a sign that God is with us. The darkness will recede. I'm a witness to that. I know that without God, I wouldn't be here right now. I certainly wouldn't be writing a book about my journey. And in the years to come, I'm sure the pain will still be there. There will still be that ache in my heart. But as the character Vision in the TV show *WandaVision* (part of the Marvel Cinematic Universe) so movingly asked, "What is grief, if not love persevering?"[2]

10

SOMETHING AND NOTHING
LIKE CLOSURE

*We know that in all things God works for
the good of those who love him, who have
been called according to his purpose.*
—Romans 8:28 NIV

I LEARNED TO BE NURTURING BECAUSE MY GRAND-
parents were nurturing. They taught me early on to always do what
I can for folks, and that's just how I roll. Plus, if it's true that kindness is contagious, I know a single act of generosity on my part has
the possibility of changing people's lives for years to come. This is
especially true if you have a platform like mine where people are
tuning in to hear your voice every morning. I know that one word of
encouragement from me, one testimony of how I'm making it after

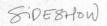

such a hard loss, will likely help someone else listening keep going. It's for that reason that I never want to stop sharing.

That same generous spirit, however, can feel like a double-edged sword, especially when people try to take advantage of it. It's a lesson I've learned the hard way, time and time again. It's not that I think I give too much. I don't believe a person *can* give too much. God loves and honors a cheerful giver, and I firmly believe that whatever I give will come back to me a hundredfold. But sometimes I do get frustrated when I give to people who I later learn take advantage of that gift. In some cases, there are people who will act as if you've never done anything good for them and speak badly about you. I've had that happen on several occasions. In other situations, there are those who start to have unhealthy expectations of your giving and can become demanding when you decide to set boundaries. I've experienced that as well. And the biggest challenge? Sometimes giving so much of myself can take away from what I need to heal.

As much as I choose to be unwavering in my commitment to helping others, I've had to learn how to be discerning in how much of myself I give. Nowadays, I do say no more often than I say yes. If I'm choosing not to do something for someone, I will at least try to point them in the direction of someone who can do it. That's my way of helping without breaching the boundaries I've set.

More than anything, though, I wonder whether being generous, being so open emotionally, is a good idea after what's happened. I wonder sometimes if being open to helping other people who are grieving keeps my wounds open. If it prevents me from getting any real closure at certain stops on this healing journey. If I'm always testifying and listening to everyone else's stories of grief and loss, if I'm always giving of myself, my money, my time, then I'm always bringing my own grief and loss back to the surface.

But what is *closure*, really? Is it even possible? After Brandon died and we got past the funeral and burial, the flood of condolences that poured in was overwhelming, to say the least. I received hundreds of messages from people all around the world, all offering their sympathies and support. And while I was grateful for each and every one of them, they also served as a reminder of the magnitude of my loss. Also, in a weird way, the outpouring shined a light on the messages I didn't receive. The people who didn't reach out. The ones I thought would be there and weren't. I'll share more about that later. But at the end of the day, through it all, one question kept nagging at me: *Can you ever truly find closure after losing a loved one?* It's a question that has haunted me in the months since my son's passing, and here's where I've landed.

I'm not sure finding closure is something we can ever really do when we've lost a child. How would that even work? Closure isn't something that just happens or that you stumble upon. In fact, we don't *find* closure at all. We create it. For me, *creating* closure has meant actively facing my grief, head-on. Allowing myself to feel every raw emotion that comes with it. That's what I share with other grieving parents. If you feel like crying, cry. Get it out of your system. Let it out. Let the tears flow.

My therapist once told me that our brains can hold all our memories and emotions, including the ones from many years ago. And even when we don't use them, they are there, like fossils, buried deep. In fact, according to researchers at NYU's Center for

Neural Science, the brain stores fear memories through a "process called memory consolidation in which an experience is captured, or encoded, then stored."[1] I know from firsthand experience that just because you don't cry doesn't mean the pain driving the tears you won't let fall isn't still there. Our brains store all these feelings, and eventually they are going to come out one way or another. For me, once I got my children and close family squared away after the funeral, I could finally give myself permission to truly mourn the loss of my son in whatever way felt right to me.

Honestly, though, I'm not even sure closure is all about grieving. I think we create closure when we find a way to honor the memory of the person we've lost. Every day that I show up to my life and live it in a way that would make my son proud, I am creating the closure I need. Every day that I stand on a stage and make people laugh, I'm creating the closure I need. In the wake of his passing, I've made it my mission not to allow the hard parts of generosity to stop me from extending a hand to anyone who needs it. Whether it's sending flowers to a grieving family or offering a shoulder to cry on, I will continue to do whatever I can to spread a little bit of light in the darkness, knowing just how much the light I've received has helped me see.

Now, I'll be the first to admit that therapy wasn't something I ever wanted to do. I've always been the kind of guy who preferred to handle things on his own. To soldier through the rough times with a smile on my face. But losing a child changes you in ways you never could have imagined. It shakes you to your core, leaving behind a void that feels impossible to fill. That's where therapy comes in. It's like a life preserver. When I talk to my therapist, I know I am in a safe space to explore whatever complicated emotions might have shown up for me that week. I can unpack the grief and anger and regret that come with my loss.

While it's changing a little bit, there are still parts of the Black community where it's hard to help people understand the benefits of therapy. We don't want to talk to nobody. And in the Black church, the stigma can be even worse. We are taught to just pray about our pain and trauma. We are supposed to *just* leave it in God's hands. We are indirectly told that if we are still feeling the pain of grief, then somehow, we don't have enough faith. But I know from my experience that this is categorically untrue. My faith is what drives me to my therapist's office. I don't ever have to divorce my trust in God from my need to receive help from someone who actually knows how the brain works, who knows how the body responds to emotional pain. Both things can be true. I can love God and pray for my healing. I can also go to a professional who God uses to help me along the way.

Going to therapy, and encouraging my children to go to therapy, is one way I've regularly and actively tried to create closure. Therapy isn't about being weak or broken. Not at all. For anyone struggling to heal from trauma or loss, who might be feeling like they are drowning, therapy is a lifeline. It's an avenue I believe God uses to, as the Bible says, "[heal] the brokenhearted and [bind] up [our] wounds" (Psalm 147:3). So I do encourage you not to be afraid to talk to someone.

Do I believe that Jesus is the ultimate therapist? Of course I do. In Matthew 11:28–30, He said, "Come to me, all you who are weary and burdened, and I will give you rest. Take my yoke upon you and learn from me, for I am gentle and humble in heart, and you will find rest for your souls. For my yoke is easy and my burden is light" (NIV). But I also think this same Bible passage is modeling for us a way we can approach our worries and grief in real time. Who else can we bring our burdens to and lay them down? A therapist might be a good starting place.

We create closure when we are generous with our time. We create it in therapy. And I think part of creating closure for ourselves when we are holding so much grief is remembering that even in the darkness of despair, there is a purpose.

It's hard to hear that our grief has a purpose. We push back against the idea that God might use our pain for good because that feels wrong. And I get it. But if we believe that God is with us through the ups and downs of life and we also believe that God is good, then why wouldn't we believe that God, in His awareness of all the things we go through, will somehow, as the ultimate Creator, transform our pain into something useful for us?

I really don't think this is the same thing as believing God causes our pain. I can't bring myself to believe that God "took my son," even though that's the language some people use as a way to make sense of things. The old church folks used to say, "God wanted him back home." Or they might say, "Well, you loved him, but God loved him best." I kind of understand this because, in their own way, people are trying to reckon with this terrible thing that has happened. It's a way to comprehend the incomprehensible.

Yet I question whether this is true, given our free will. We get to make our own choices. I've got to believe that when we make a choice that leads to our demise, the people who are left behind are comforted by God. It's not that God inflicts pain upon us, but rather, He stands ready to offer solace and comfort through the indwelling of His Spirit.

Nevertheless, this reassurance does little to ease the rawness of our grief. It doesn't make it feel good. Which is why some people might even resist the good that's born from the pain—because they don't feel worthy of it. They don't feel like they should embrace anything good because of the loss they experienced. But I choose to believe that any positive outcome since the loss of my son is a reflection of Brandon's desires for me. I believe he is now part of that great cloud of witnesses who are rooting me on as I grow from this experience. He's wanting joy and love and peace for me.

I choose to believe all this because to entertain any other narrative would be to invite devastation of unimaginable proportions. And at the end of the day, all we have is our faith. All we have is what we believe. Even those who don't believe in God believe in something. Those without faith cling to something amid deep grief. For me, faith is my anchor when nothing else makes sense. It is what I cling to.

Again, I don't ever want to pretend like holding on to faith and trusting that good can come from loss is easy. It's not. But I've seen where a person has lost a family member, even a child, and has gone

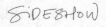

on to preach their greatest sermon or grow their business in a way they never had before. I've seen people transform their pain into a book that blesses millions of people or a chart-topping song that resonates with folks who have gone through similar issues. It's so important for us to be open to what God might do. To believe that God can orchestrate something good from the pain.

That kind of hope is healing. While it will never erase the ache of loss or bring back our loved ones, it offers a pathway to healing. If we can experience the greatest loss of our lives and still have a little hope that something beautiful will come from the experience, then why not embrace that? No, it won't bring Brandon back. Hope won't bring our loved ones back. But it can be a salve that will help us, in the long run, to heal from the challenges of the past and emotional turmoil sure to come. The grief process is filled with twists and turns, highs and lows—that much is clear. Yet there exists a thread of divine purpose, weaving its way through the fabric of our pain. God can take the broken pieces of our hearts and fashion them into something beautiful.

Romans 8:28 says, "We know that in all things God works for the good of those who love him, who have been called according to his purpose" (NIV). This verse reminds me that Brandon's passing, as devastating as it may be, was not in vain. Through faith and perseverance and support, we can find meaning and purpose even when we're in the most pain. As I've said over and over again on these pages, I'm not sure grief is something we get over. I think it's something that just gets integrated into our lives. It becomes part of us. Part of creating closure is accepting that there really isn't any closure to be had. At least not in the sense that there is an ending to my experience, a destination that I somehow arrive at on this healing journey, or a point in time when I won't remember. I will always remember.

I just wish more people knew that.

As much as family and friends have lent me their shoulders to cry on, their ears to listen, or given me a hug when I needed it, there are many who showed their true colors at the worst possible time. That's important for you to know also. In fact, if you've been through a loss, chances are you've seen it too. People who turn your memories into machetes and try to cut you with them. People who don't know how to hold their own grief and pain and so they lash out at you. People who use your loss as a way to hurt you. You might find yourself looking around and wondering what is happening. Why are people acting out the way they are, at such a difficult time? What do you do about that when it happens? Well, sometimes it's necessary to start with calling a thing, a thing. To name what is happening. For me, I've come to realize that there can't be a story of healing from loss without sharing the sometimes-ugly parts of how loss can play out in families. How I've been treated since he died. When Black church folks say, "But God . . ." and they leave the rest of that phrase hanging, this is what I think about. All the ways I felt abandoned, and how God filled in the gaps.

11

THE INSULT TO THE INJURY

What hurts us is what heals us.
—Paulo Coelho

LET ME TELL YOU A RAW, UNFILTERED TRUTH: THERE
have been so many times since Brandon died when I've felt totally
abandoned by those close to me. That was real. Could that feeling
have been born from a grief that blinds me from seeing anything
other than my own pain? Maybe. I'll own that, if it is true. But I
cannot deny that some things that happened during this time didn't
feel so good.

In the months after the funeral, it was strange to sometimes
sit in my house and be aware of the silence. To not hear the laughter that used to fill the room. I was lonelier and felt emptier, not
because Brandon wasn't here anymore but because of the absence
of those I thought would stand by me in my darkest hour. As much

as there was a groundswell of support from strangers—fans and followers—as well as the presence of my immediate family, so many people seemed to vanish into thin air. And even within my family, I felt a distance I never had before Brandon died. My mother, bless her heart, immersed herself in church and ministry, which I don't blame her for. It was probably the only way she could deal with her own grief, but man, sometimes you just need your people. And not always just to cry with you or hold you either. There were some days when I just wanted to feel the warmth of someone's presence. Or to know that someone was thinking about me. Especially since the ones who meant the world to me, who I know would have held me and loved me through all this, my grandparents, were no longer around.

Brandon's death amplified just how much I miss my grandparents. They may not have had all the right words, but they knew how to show love. The Monday after my first grandma, my mom's mom, died, my other grandparents said to me, "Hey, come on over here now. Come on over and get something to eat!" Then, when I got there, my grandmother sat on the couch and opened a book with nothing but newspaper clippings from various shows I'd done.

"I got all your stuff right here," she said. "We just want you to know that we really love you and we are really proud of you." That tore me up right on the spot. I started crying. That's when my granddaddy said, "Don't do that. Come on now. Don't do that. You're going to be fine. You don't want your grandmama down here suffering, do you?"

That same day, my granddaddy fixed me a plate of food for the first time ever. Listen, he was from a different time. In his era, men didn't make their own plates, much less somebody else's. But he did that for me. And that simple act showed me just how much he loved me. All my grandparents had a way of making me feel seen, even when the world felt like it was closing in on me. These elders knew how to show up when it mattered most. They were always reminding me that I was loved and valued.

But now, in this season of grief, when I expected that same kind of care from the people who really know me, it's actually been the unexpected ones who've shown up. High school classmates, old friends, even folks I barely knew were the ones who reached out to me with words of comfort.

"What you need, Rick?" they'd say.

"I'm coming through after your show—what you want me to bring you?" they'd ask.

It's funny how sometimes it's the people you least expect who come through for you when you need it most. When Brandon died, people I hadn't talked to in years called to check on me. Friends from my old neighborhood in Birmingham. Some who came all the way from Jacksonville or down from Detroit. I heard more from Sybrina Fulton, Trayvon Martin's mother; Le'Andria Johnson; Darlene McCoy; Smokie Norful; and different pastors from all over the country than from people who lived down the street. It's funny . . . and sad. But you know what? Maybe that's the lesson. Blood ain't always thicker than water. For many reasons. Sometimes, it's the family you choose, the friends who become like family, who hold you up when you can't stand on your own. And maybe, just maybe, there's a bit of grace in recognizing that not everyone has the capacity to show up the way you need them to. They might be so

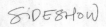

wrapped up in their own sorrow that they can't see past it to anyone else's pain. We're all just doing the best we can with what we've got.

———————

But here's the hard part: some people just don't have the inner generosity, the inner capacity, to look beyond themselves. For a person like me who does spend inordinate amounts of time putting my pain aside to take care of others, it stings when those same people don't seem to give a damn. It feels like an insult to the injury.

In 2022, right before Brandon passed away, I hosted not one but two Thanksgiving dinners on the same day. Why? Because I wanted to make sure that everyone got a chance to eat and fellowship with the people they love. And the Easter after Brandon passed in 2023, I did something similar. I desperately wanted to inject some happiness into our lives, gather everyone together, and reminisce about better days. I had a big Easter egg hunt for the kids and let everyone who came to the funeral spend the night at the house. A bunch of younger adults from among friends and family were there. I wanted it to be a really nice weekend, but I later learned that it was something else entirely. Little did I know, folks were smoking weed in my driveway. This was unbelievable. Hurtful. Knowing how we lost Brandon, these people I'd helped raise showed blatant disrespect in my home. When I did find out about it, I was angry.

Father's Day weekend rolled around, and I decided to try again with a get-together at the house. Do you think anything changed? No. I mean, who throws up in a blanket and hides it in the dirty laundry? *That's a new level of low*, I thought. A family friend who helps me around the house found it while cleaning up the mess left by somebody's drunken antics. Needless to say, all this put a strain on my relationships.

It's not just about me, though. It's really about respect. I'd expected a kind of reverence for the mourning period. You just don't do the same things you might have done three years ago at a party. Even as a kid, I knew to act a little differently because my grandparents were actively mourning. And yet there I was, dealing with all this drama.

I'd been there for folks through thick and thin. But when I needed them most, too many of them let me down. Brandon's death opened my eyes to who truly had my back and who was just along for the ride. I had tried to support them, gave them opportunities, and what did I get in return? Disrespect, betrayal, and silence.

For the longest time, I felt like I didn't need their empty apologies. I just wanted their changed behavior. If you're truly sorry, show it through your actions, right? Otherwise, keep your apologies to yourself. *Forgiveness is earned, not freely given*, I thought.

Then it dawned on me.

Who forgave me when I absolutely didn't deserve it?

Who paid the price for my sin?

Yeah, exactly.

You see there?

Two things are once again true. I was well within my rights to want to be treated with respect. And the people in my life also might absolutely *not* know how to do that, and all while trying to grieve Brandon's loss themselves.

I finally got the message God was sending my way.

I figured out that when it comes to this grief thing, there are some people who cannot or will not hold the weight of my sorrow. So much so that they will act out in order to resist doing so. They can barely hold the weight of their own.

I also learned that I could not expect people to do what I would do for them. Which is hard, you know? Because I'm human. And it's a real human thing to want some kind of reciprocation of your love and attention. It's not easy to be sitting in a big ol' house by yourself, crying, and thinking about the hundreds of meals you've cooked for people. How they came over and enjoyed your swimming pool and movie theater, but when you really need them, the house is quiet. But I now know that if I allow the lack of reciprocation to continue to make me angry or frustrated or otherwise upset, I have to check my own motivations for doing for these people in the first place. And while it can't be about "what I did for them," I do get to decide how to proceed knowing that those I'd hoped would be there for me, couldn't be.

I decided not to get angry about it anymore. I chose not to stay upset. I simply protected my heart and peace. And I decided to be more discerning about how I extended myself.

When the next Thanksgiving holiday came around, I strongly considered not hosting. I wasn't feeling up to it, and I couldn't help but not want any fair-weather friends wining and dining in my house when they couldn't be bothered to check on me at all as I mourned my son. But I knew that would cause a stir. Like, a full-on church split in the family. And I didn't want that either. Yes, life would have gone on. Folks would have eaten elsewhere. I would have probably rested. But I just couldn't bring myself to do that. Hey, I'm still learning.

My next decision was to just believe myself to be unique. Different. I think differently about how we should treat people even when we're experiencing pain. Maybe it comes from the way I grew up. I watched how the people around me extended themselves to help others even when they were going through a hard time. So my approach is like that. If someone is hurting, I'm not going to be quiet. I'm not always going to "give them space." I'm going to do what I can to help. There have been times when I've gotten on Facebook Messenger and talked to people, absolute strangers, about the loss of their child. Parents have called me at three and four o'clock in the morning, right when they found out their child has died, and I not only answered the phone, but I stayed up with them until they had to leave. "No, ma'am, you're good. You're not bothering me. I'm just going to the radio station. But there ain't nothing wrong with my mouth. I can talk. I can talk to you all the way to the radio station." The way I've chosen to deal with doing all I do and not getting that same love and respect in return is believing that this is my ministry now, and God will honor it.

Listen, as much as I could rail against the people who didn't show up for me when Brandon died, I know that the best thing for my healing is to focus on the ones who did. And to continue to modify my life as needed to this new normal I'm living. For the ones who checked on me, and who continue to check on my heart, I

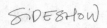

am forever grateful. But also, I've realized lately that it's not just about them checking on me. It's also about me being vulnerable enough to ask for help when I need it. That's the main thing that has helped me feel better about these perceived slights.

The saying goes, "Check on your strong friends," and I get it. There are those of us who people think don't need help. They believe we don't need a lot of care. They see us functioning and surviving and think, *Oh well, Rickey got it all together.* And usually, that's as far from the truth as it could be. Most of the time we are simply being strong to cover up just how much pain we are actually holding. But I also think we "strong friends" have to be accountable to ourselves too. How many times have I needed someone to speak life into me, but at the same time, I wanted them to just know that and call me instead of me picking up the phone and sharing what I need and how they can help? Maybe friends like that aren't fair-weather at all. Maybe they just see us as a pillar of strength and don't believe there is anything they can add to make things better. They are wrong, for sure. But if we aren't asking for help, maybe we should own our part in our own loneliness.

We may have to reach out to our friends and let them know what we need, but there's a big part of me that feels like family should just know to do what needs to be done. They're family, right? Take my mother, for instance. I know she loves me. I know she means well. But sometimes, all she's had to offer me are Bible verses when really what I needed were her words of love and care. Now, don't get me wrong, I respect the power of the Word of God to heal, but there were times when I felt so low about Brandon that I needed her to be a mom, not a preacher. But again, I'm not holding that against her.

Not anymore. We all have our baggage, and people handle trauma differently. I know my mother took Brandon's death hard. She had been doing everything she knew how to do to help him when he died. Not to mention that not too long after Brandon passed, I had to tell my mother about my uncle, her brother, passing away.

Man, life is so freaking fragile. You don't realize that until you get slapped around a few times by it. I suspect Mama is doing everything she can to maintain her own sobriety in the midst of all this loss. Hiding behind the cross might be the only way she can deal with her own grief. So I can't be mad at that. Life is too short. I'm watching so many of my friends deal with the passing of their mothers. I know I'm blessed to still have mine. I must accept the fact that she is doing the best she can with what she's got mentally and emotionally. She is giving me the best she has to offer.

As I said, though, there were those who showed up when it mattered most, and I'm doing my best to focus my attention on them. Like my adopted nephew, Brandon Conner, and his wife, who were grilling some sliders one day and randomly invited me over.

"Come on over here and eat," they said. "We don't care what you got to do. You better come on and eat." I was making excuses about not coming because I was tired and sad, but they didn't accept a single one. They made me come, and I'm so glad I went.

My classmates from Woodlawn High School and my chapter brothers from the Alpha Phi chapter of Omega Psi Phi ushered and parked cars at Brandon's funeral. Friends like Chef Kirk Boudreaux and other comedians like DC Young Fly and Chico Bean were all in my text messages asking, "You good?"

The Wednesday after Brandon died, I was getting ready to go to bed after a long day. I'd done my morning show and then served food to the homeless at the Salvation Army. Serving that food was the one way I knew how to keep myself together. It was my way of letting God know that even though my boy was gone, like Job, I was not going to curse Him. Just as I was about to lie down, I saw a car pull up my driveway. It was my friend from the fifth grade at the door. One I'd stood next to when he buried his own son. When he walked in, I said, "Go on over to the bar; I will make you a drink." He said he came over to just sit with me.

That's it. Sit with me.

I made him a drink and that's what we did. We just sat there. It blessed me so much. That's what the ministry of presence looks like. No fancy words, just being there.

And then there were all my friends who'd been through their own losses. They were there for me, just like I was for them. That's real love, deep and unwavering.

Can this part of the grief journey get lonely? Hell yeah. There's no denying that. But I've learned that in those moments when the silence is deafening, you really do just have to trust God. Because when you are trusting God, He gives you the strength to lean on yourself when you can't lean on anyone else. Like the song says, sometimes I have to "encourage myself."[1] I have to remind myself that I'm special, just like my granddaddy used to say.

Here's the truth: in your darkest moments, the true colors of those around you will shine through, revealing who has the capacity to stand firm and who will falter under the weight of your grief. It will feel like betrayal. Especially if you have been the one who has supported and lifted others up in their time of need. But it will help to remember that not everyone possesses the fortitude or empathy to extend you a hand of support. They just don't. And that will have to be okay. In those times when loneliness has settled in and grief won't let you go and there's no one reaching out and no one for you to call, open your mouth and cry out to God. I promise you, He hears you. I promise you, He's not sitting high and judging your pain. I promise you, He's not expecting you to know what to do and how to do it. The Spirit of the living God will sit with you even when no one else will. If you let Him.

Then, after crying out to God and trusting Him to be there for you, it's important to take control of your own narrative. Never let the actions of others dictate your happiness. Feel what you feel, but try to live life with peace and dignity and leave behind anything or anyone who chooses to disrupt that.

Finally, forgive them. Forgive the ones who, after you lost your loved one, hurt you. Left you. Talked about you. As I've said, I know what that feels like. It wasn't just the absence of certain people that stung the most when Brandon died—it was the betrayal, the abandonment, the utter disregard for my pain. Yes, there were those who chose to turn a blind eye to my pain. Those who, out of their own grief, disrespected me and my home. And then there were those who actively sought to undermine me, to sow seeds of discord in the fertile soil of grief. Their issues were festering long before Brandon died, and this was the moment they popped out.

One lady I knew always seemed to revel in emasculating me and loved to tear me down at every opportunity. When Brandon passed, she saw it as her chance to strike, to drive a wedge in my family in the name of her own twisted agenda. When I was struggling with my oldest daughter and dealing with our arguments, she whipped them up. In other instances, she picked fights with me about random things that made no sense.

Then, at the funeral home, during the viewing, I thought she was going to get on my very last nerve. She did everything possible to be seen. She kept getting up and moving around for no reason. My thing was, if you know you're already not in a good space with me, please sit down. Be still. Let me know that you're here and ready to help, but stay out of everyone's face. But that would have been asking too much.

There was also an old coworker who seemed to make every tragic thing that happened to my family about her. She spoke publicly about my losses, which might have been fine if she'd actually reached out to me first. But she never did. Never reached out to say I'm sorry or anything. But when one of her family members passed away, I put our beef aside, threw on my suit, and drove many hours to the funeral to pay my respects.

All of this enraged me. And hurt. To have someone I once called family or friend try to kick me when I'm down? That's hard. It's the reason why, in the wake of Brandon's passing, I've grappled so much with that same forgiveness I'm suggesting for you—forgiving those who abandoned you, who betrayed your trust, who added insult to injury in your darkest hour. It's a process, to be sure—one filled with pain and resentment—but ultimately, it's a necessary step on the road to healing.

Forgiveness does not only benefit the person who hurt us. It also brings us the peace we are longing for. It requires us to surrender our need to make something right that isn't ours to make right in the first place. It allows us to leave those people in God's hands and embrace the grace that comes our way when we extend that same grace to others. It's a challenge, but it's worth it in the end.

There is a part of me that knows that because I've experienced all this heartache from those close to me, God gives me an enormous amount of love from elsewhere. I truly believe that. It's as if He said, *Okay, family, you want to trip on Rickey? Well, I'm going to let him be loved by thousands of other people.* It's like He truly gives me double for my trouble, without fail. But even so, there are days in this healing process when I don't want to wait to be justified. I want to be able to forgive and move on. I want to find peace within myself and with those I have conflict with. In the meantime, I just keep praying for a win.

PART THREE

I AM HEALING

*A happy heart is good medicine and
a joyful mind causes healing,
But a broken spirit dries up the bones.*
PROVERBS 17:22 AMP

12

LET THE TEARS FALL

*Grief is a very living thing. I tried to work
it away. I tried to drink it away. And all
it did was wait for me to finish.*
—Tyler Perry

THE FIRST TIME I ALLOWED MYSELF TO SHED REAL
tears and release even a little of the pain I felt from losing Brandon
was the Wednesday after he passed. As I've shared, I went to work.
I did it, despite radio station execs telling me to "take as much time
off as I need." But I knew that would not be good for me.

"Either I'm on the air Wednesday," I said, "or I'm going to be
lying in bed, broken and replaying every bit of regret and hurt in
my head."

And that was something I absolutely didn't want to do. I *needed*
to occupy my mind. A part of me also thought that if I went to work,

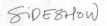

I would be able to push down any extreme emotional responses. I thought I'd be able to hold my tears, but God had other plans. He wasn't going to let me get away from the release I so desperately needed.

During the show, I do what I call a praise break. This is where we play gospel music and I try to offer a word of encouragement for the audience. My goal is always to help set the tone of their day. That Wednesday, I opened with the praise break as usual—this time also streaming live on Facebook. At one point, a song—I don't even remember which one—just hit me square in my heart. That's when I got up from my chair and lay on the floor screaming and crying. It was like every feeling I'd held in for those three days since I got the news came pouring out of me. It also felt like God was catching every tear. It was like He was reminding me of David's words in Psalm 56:8, "You keep track of all my sorrows. You have collected all my tears in your bottle. You have recorded each one in your book" (NLT).

Once I experienced that first release, I periodically would shed a quiet tear here and there. Walking into the church for Brandon's funeral and seeing his picture on those jumbotrons made my soul ache. Taking in the looks on everyone's faces, especially his mom's and grandma's, made my heart break. But there was still nothing as big as that day in the studio until after the funeral when we were at the cemetery. It tore me up from the inside out to see my boy lowered into the ground. I wailed. But then God, in His infinite wisdom, gave my heart a respite. A little rest until the next wave. It's like my body was easing me into this life of grief I now have.

Like the heavens knew I could handle only brief spikes in emotion as opposed to a constant avalanche.

The next time grief wrenched those big, heavy tears out of me was right before a show in Cleveland, my first performance after Brandon passed. From the time I left my hotel room, I just felt sad. There was this heavy despair hovering over me, especially as I realized that I was doing the show by myself. Brandon wasn't there. None of the kids were there. I felt so alone. My auntie Brim lived in Cleveland at the time and, while she was coming to the show already, I suppose I could have spent more time with her family. But I didn't want to bring my heaviness to her kids and grandkids. They would inevitably sense something was not right. Plus, I knew my auntie played no games about me. When she heard about Brandon, she'd immediately said, "We're on our way to Birmingham." But I told her not to come. I didn't want her to spend too much of her resources making the trip. I knew her heart. I knew she loved me and Brandon. That was enough. So if Auntie Brim knew just how broken I was before the show, I know she would have pulled out all the stops to try to make me feel okay. I couldn't have that. I wasn't even sure I *wanted* to feel okay.

When I got into the car that evening to head over to Harrah's Casino, the venue for the show, I looked at the driver and something came over me. Waves of grief hit me hard. I know he must have thought I was crazy because there I was, in his car, the star of this show that was happening in less than an hour, bawling my eyes out in the back seat. After letting out a bloodcurdling scream, I could feel the tension in the air as the poor guy didn't know what to do.

But there was nothing he could do. People see you cry or scream or otherwise feel the weight of your loss and, with good intentions, they want you to stop. They don't want you to feel bad. But that doesn't make sense. A bad thing has happened. A painful thing has happened. And as human beings, we get to feel what we feel. Otherwise, how else will we move through it? The hard truth is, people want us to stop the outward demonstrations of grief mostly because it makes *them* uncomfortable. They find themselves feeling a bit helpless at not being able to do anything to assist us, and so they stumble over themselves trying to make something right that can't be righted—not realizing that the best thing they could ever do is just be present. Silent but present goes a long way toward helping grieving folks manage those waves.

When we finally pulled up to the venue, I stayed in the car and cried. Then I got myself together to go in, headed backstage, and cried some more. Then I dried my face and walked onto the stage.

"Put your hands together for Riiickey Smiiiiileeeeey!"

I had the best revelation that night before the Cleveland show as I looked out at the sold-out crowd in the casino. Seeing all those people—many of whom followed the radio show and knew about my loss—showing up for me was mind-blowing. It flipped a switch in me. God used them that night to say, *Rickey, you must keep going somehow. It's hard. And heavy. And painful. But I'm here. Keep going.*

Grief hits you at the weirdest times. And it's especially hard and strange if you already tend to be an empathetic person. You not only feel your pain, but you feel the pain of everyone around you. At the funeral, I didn't even realize my youngest son, Malik, was feeling pain to the degree he was until we all got into the church. I was down on my knees playing with my grandbaby when Darlene McCoy, singer, radio personality, and friend who once said I was "built Ford tough," got up to sing "I Love the Lord" by Richard Smallwood. That's when I heard the commotion and saw D'essence and Aaryn trying to comfort Malik. But he wasn't responding to anyone, so I got out of my seat and went over to him.

"Hey, hey. It's okay. Stand up," I said. Once he heard my voice, he seemed to lock in. Then we stood in the aisle together and I started rubbing his back. That's when he started to scream. And I felt every bit of his anguish. Malik started stomping up and down that aisle. "Let it out, Malik," I said. "It's okay, scream it out." And I meant that. But it still felt like we were standing in front of a firing squad. In that moment, all I could do was drop to my knees and pray for help.

"God, please help us. God, please. What is this? What is all of this? What's going on?"

Sometimes prayer is all I have. Like Darlene said, I'm certainly tough. But it's not about being tough all the time. The people who are the toughest on the outside also tend to be the ones who hurt the most on the inside. Yes, there are times I can't feel all my feelings. When it's time to lead, you lead. The time when Malik was a baby and had a high fever to the point where he went into convulsions, I didn't have the luxury of panicking. His mom was screaming—was I going to scream too? No. A temperature means your body is hot, so I ran into the bathroom, got a towel, and ran some ice-cold water on it. Then I wrapped him up in that cold towel and it kept the fever down until the ambulance arrived. My job in that moment was to focus on saving his life. I cried later, but

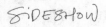

in the moment, I had to be there for my son. The same goes with Brandon's death. I didn't have the luxury of crying and wailing in front of his siblings and the rest of the family. They were hurting enough, and I didn't want to add to it. But that suppression could not last for too long.

I believe it's okay to press pause for a little while, but at some point, very soon after, we all must release the pain. Maybe it's crying with abandon. Maybe it's screaming into the woods. Maybe it's running until you can't anymore. Whatever it looks like, it must happen. Or the pain will eat you up inside. When those waves of grief hit, don't run from them. If it's safe enough to do so, let those emotions do what they're going to do. Ride it out. And when it finally passes, keep living. Until the next time.

There will always be things that cause us to remember the person we lost. Waves of grief can be triggered by even the smallest reminders. We don't have to run from those memories, though. I'm of the mind that we should lean into those triggers, especially when the recollections are good ones. I've seen people who can't bring themselves to look at pictures of their loved one or who are devastated when Facebook memories or Timehop images from a year or two or five ago pop up on their news feeds. It can be troubling to see an image of your child after you've lost them. In the first year or so, it can be hard. But once we move further along the grief process, it can be a good thing, a way to access more joy, when we lean into those good memories. There is also a profound opportunity for healing—to allow the memories to serve as a reminder of the life we once shared with our loved one. By embracing these triggers, we get to remember that this person was part of our lives. They lived.

It doesn't matter if it was five years or fifty—they were on this earth, and every day they were here mattered. And if that's true, the memories that make up those days are actually ones we should treasure—not walk away from.

Ease your way into this, though. In the initial days of grief, the prospect of revisiting cherished memories may seem unbearable, so take whatever time you need. It might not be the first month or two. Maybe even not the first year. Move at your own pace, but keep your eyes on one day being able to get to the place where you can hold those glorious memories. The first time she took her first step. The moment he jumped out of the swing and thought he was flying. The time he walked across the stage and picked up his high school diploma. The moment she had her first child. One way to begin mending a broken heart is to realize that the length of our lives matters less than the quality of our lives.

The catch to all of this is that we often don't get to choose which memories come up for us. We won't be able to dictate what resurfaces, nor can we shield ourselves from the pain that accompanies the painful memories.

After Brandon died, I received an honorary doctorate degree from Miles College. They asked me to be the commencement speaker, and it was one of the hardest things I've ever had to do. Not because of the speech. I was totally fine with that. It was because I was watching these students get their degrees and remembering the day I took Brandon to college. I could see his face in the faces of the men who walked that stage. I could see my nephew Ron too. The memories just flooded me. There have been so many moments just like that. Events that remind me of what might have been.

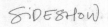

Sometimes I can't do anything but cry. Other days I lean into the feeling. I accept the form grief is taking.

It would be nice if only the good memories showed up. It would be nice if it was only the positive, joyful memories of Brandon that came up for me. But that's not the case. Whenever we lean into the memories that trigger any emotion in us, we're bound to come across the ones that are not so great. Which is why we have to be equipped to manage those feelings too.

This is where the support of a village is a big deal. Having the support of family, close friends, or a therapist can really help you reclaim your grief process because they will be able to help you weed through the images and sort through the more painful memories and put them in their proper place. Many therapists talk about creating a container in your mind where you can place certain thoughts. I like the idea of that. When hard memories come up, you can put them into a container in your mind. You don't throw them away because, for real, you actually can't. They're always going to be there. They are the reality of the life this person lived. But putting them in your mental container means they don't have to take over. You can choose where you place your attention. You can focus on the positive memories. The ones you want to keep and treasure for the rest of your life.

So yes, there will always be triggers. Good and bad. Things that will cause grief to rise in your body, mind, and heart. As I've said, music is one for me. Certain songs can take me there if I allow myself to float on the melodies and feel everything. The changing of the seasons is another trigger for me. It's as though the passage of time is a reminder of what we've lost. But now the tears come easier.

The release is more frequent and intentional. Just last week I cried so much I could have floated away on my tears.

I've even had moments of absentmindedness that have given me some of the most releasing laughter of my life. When the mother of one of my classmates, Tawana, was diagnosed with cancer, I went over to see the woman. After our conversation, something in my spirit told me I wasn't going to see her again. And I was right. She passed away shortly after my visit. When I got the news, there was no question whether I was going to support my friend through this loss.

"When is the funeral?" I asked.

"Saturday at twelve o'clock," she said.

"Okay, I'm going to go help coach my grandson's football game and then come right over."

I threw my clothes in the car, and after the game, I ran over to the church. When I arrived, I saw that people were mingling in the lobby and figured that it was the family hour where members of the family can view the deceased before the actual service. So when everyone started to line up, I did too. I didn't have time to change so I just laid my clothes on the back pew, took an obituary program, and sat down. I didn't go up to the casket. I wasn't ready to do that after Brandon's funeral. But I was there and glad to be. While seated, I saw two of my classmates and thought, *Okay, I'm good. Didn't miss anything.*

That first part of the service was powerful, and I even found myself crying as I watched the family honor this amazing woman. I'm sure my own grief was triggered because I cried so much even the funeral directors were fanning me. One of the nurses said, "Do y'all think he need a cold rag?"

After a while, though, something didn't feel right. I didn't see Tawana anywhere. That's when I texted her.

"You all okay?"

I looked at the front row to see if I saw anyone looking at their phone. No one. That's when a sinking feeling came over me.

I texted Tawana again.

"I think I'm at the wrong funeral. New Rising Star, right?"

Then those dreaded three dots appeared on my phone. She was texting me back.

"Are you serious? New MORNING Star."

Oh.

I turned to the funeral directors and nurses and said, "I'm at the wrong funeral. I'm supposed to be at New Morning Star." Then I walked out of the church with my clothes in my hand.

You want to talk about embarrassed? Those same funeral directors laughed so hard at me, they were practically on the ground as I left. Two of them were leaning over the rail crying real tears of laughter.

But that wasn't the end of the hilarity that ensued that day.

Thank God the service I was supposed to be at was only seven minutes away. I flew over to the other church, parked, and decided to change my clothes in the car. As soon as I stripped all the way down to my drawers, two of my classmates came up to the car to say hi. Startled by me being nearly naked, they burst out laughing and walked away.

But wait, there's more.

I got dressed and grabbed my keys and the obituary for the service. I was ready, right? Sure. I walked into the service, sat down, and looked at the obituary in my hands. Yep, it was for the woman at the other church. When I started shaking my head at the absolute ridiculousness of it all, two more of my classmates who were also sitting in the last two rows asked me what was wrong.

"I done went to the wrong funeral," I said.

Their response?

Yep, they all fell out laughing. I mean, every single one of them was down bad. Even my friend, who knew what happened, didn't let it go. When she and her husband came up to all of us afterward, we hugged each other. Then she looked at me and said, "I hear another obituary got brought in the mix."

I can be all right, doing what I do, and somehow a reminder comes in the form of a whisper in my head. *Brandon has passed*, it says. There are still moments when I think, *This can't be real.* Nearly every day, actually. It's almost like Brandon dies every day. That same deep, butterfly-like anxiety I felt in the early days returns. I could be having a good day, but something still feels off. Rotten. And for a brief moment, I might be confused about what it is. Then it's like, "Oh. That."

I think this is why it's so important for me to continue telling jokes and making people laugh. Why I'm okay with crying my eyes out one minute and laughing onstage the next. On the stage, I have found a sanctuary where my grief and joy coexist. Every joke told, each punch line delivered, revives me in a way. Yes, my journey has been punctuated by moments that have tested my strength and

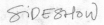

resolve—the loss of loved ones, the weight of grief, and the relentless pursuit of this work I feel called to do. But in the midst of tears and laughter, I've learned to endure. The stages I've graced, from small clubs to grand auditoriums, are sacred spaces for me. Sure, people come to my shows to laugh. But I also think they come to my shows to release some stuff. To heal.

I know people say this about more traditional types of art—dance, music, painting—but I believe that comedy has the ability to transmute pain into beauty as well. To turn sorrow into a source of strength. As I stand on the stage, I am not just a comedian. I am a storyteller. I get to commune with my audiences. And the communal act of sharing laughter in a crowded room binds us. Every show is a reminder that joy is not out there. It's inside me. Inside all of us. Joy is a choice we make. A signal to the world that we will fight to find our light.

Every joke I tell, every roast I deliver, in a weird way, offers a reprieve from the pain. And in that relief, repair can come. Healing can come. And if healing comes, then I can keep pushing, keep going. For me, at this point in my life, if I don't cry until I laugh, then I cannot help folks laugh until they cry.

13

GOT ME SOME GRATITUDE

How lucky I am to have something that
makes saying goodbye so hard.
—Winnie the Pooh

"HE'S AT PEACE, RICKEY," SHE SAID.

I'm so grateful for Miss Jannie, a family friend who has helped me with my children over the years. She was friends with my grandparents and someone with whom I've developed a good relationship.

"God came and got him because he was sick."

My first response was, *What?!*

In my mind, I was thinking that this was just something old people said. Because they were set in their ways. But then she went on.

"You need to let that boy go," she said firmly.

When Brandon first passed, Miss Jannie was like a guardian

angel here on earth for me. When she saw how heavy grief was sitting on me, she called me over to her house. As soon as I walked through the door, she told me to sit down as she locked the door and took the phone off the hook. Then she proceeded to deliver a message I didn't know I needed.

"He's in a better place."

Her words sank down deep. Deeper than even the resistance I felt at hearing them.

"God's got him."

It wasn't like she didn't know what she was talking about. Like she hadn't lived what I was going through. Miss Jannie had lost two of her sons, a year and a half apart.

"He ain't suffering anymore, but you're not going to be okay until you let him go."

That's when it clicked. For some reason, those words resonated with me.

"Do you hear me?" she said.

"Yes, ma'am," I said.

That was it. Miss Jannie's words settled into my heart, mingling with the raw ache of loss that wasn't going anywhere anytime soon. They were like a balm. A healing agent she poured down on me thick and heavy. It hasn't been an easy journey toward acceptance. Not by a long shot. But Miss Jannie's guidance planted a seed of gratitude within me. It made me realize that even in the pain and sorrow, it's possible to find light. The light in my loss was that Brandon was no longer struggling with addiction. He was no longer suffering with whatever drove him to it. My boy is free, and that is something to be thankful for.

Of course, it wasn't magic. I didn't just—*poof*—let the death of my boy go completely in that moment. But that time with Miss Jannie was a turning point for me. I was able to start releasing a little bit because those words made me cry. I sat there on her couch and cried like a baby. Until, of course, Miss Jannie said, "Nope. Stop it. Don't start all that crying now."

There's something about our elders and the wisdom they share. I know it's a trendy thing to disregard the past nowadays. To throw aside the life lessons our parents, grandparents, and great-grandparents can offer, in favor of some weird disconnect in our understanding of what independence truly is. When folks talk about not needing the past or talk down about what our ancestors did or didn't do, I already know they aren't all that wise. They see independence through the lens of individualism and isolation. But that's not how I grew up. That's not how many of us grew up, especially if you were Black and in the South. We intuitively understand that the more we turn *toward* community, toward a more *inter*dependent way of moving through the world, the better off we are. And I think that starts with allowing our elders to speak into our lives. Will they always be right? No. Is the wisdom and guidance they offer still very valuable? Absolutely. I'm grateful for that wisdom. For how people like Miss Jannie speak life into me. And I'm grateful for the faith behind it all.

When I was experiencing the worst of my despair, moments when I couldn't even breathe right, I also experienced the presence of God like I never had before. I'm so grateful for that. Loss has a peculiar way of testing one's faith. It's a crucible that either breaks you down until you can't hold on to anything you once believed to be true, or strengthens your faith in God and all the workings of the spirit realm. In my case, it did the latter. That's why I keep repeating that God is walking through this with us. He's holding us as we move through our grief. Sure, it can be real easy to get stuck at "God, why didn't You stop this? Why did You allow this to happen?" We can once again find ourselves wallowing in the false belief that God "took" our loved one from us. Forgetting that God gave every human being free will and sometimes acting out that free will has harsh consequences. Forgetting that we cannot see into the future. We don't know if death on this side is actually a kind of salvation. But what we do know is that God never leaves us. Never forsakes us.

Jesus is a "man of sorrows" who is "acquainted with grief" (Isaiah 53:3). And that tracks for me. When the storm raged for me, when I sat in my condo after getting the news and was completely engulfed by grief, the Spirit of the living God gave me solace. Gave me just enough to take the next step and the next step and the next. God's grace was truly sufficient (2 Corinthians 12:9).

Once I embraced gratitude as the posture of my heart, God granted me other sources of comfort. Mainly from people I'd worked with, served with, or respected. My good friend, gospel music artist Smokie Norful, reached out to me with Scripture and encouragement that seemed to be perfectly timed with moments when I was wavering. He wore me out as I walked around in the backyard wondering why I was still here. Why Brandon wasn't. Those calls often breathed new life into my weary soul. Not only was God with me

172

but God had sent His people to walk alongside me when I couldn't walk this thing out very well myself.

Similarly, my pastor, Kelvin Bryant of Faith Walkers Church, continued to speak life to me one Sunday. It was an offering of vulnerability that let me know I was not alone. Having lost his own daughter, he kept it all the way real: "Man, I'd been up here preaching all these years, telling people to come to God, and when that happened, I couldn't believe that God did that to me."

Whew! I felt that in my bones.

"I know how you feel," I said.

I couldn't help but wonder why my faithfulness could not have kept this tragedy from me. It's hard not to think about why God allows bad things to happen to good people. Me and my kids are good folks. Not perfect but trying. I'd been out here doing community service. We used to get up on Christmas at 3 a.m. with a police motorcade and go through our community giving toys to kids. We did that instead of sitting up in our house opening expensive gifts. We try to be humble. Even on the reality show, we were at the Salvation Army serving the homeless. Didn't that count for anything?

Even a decade before I lost Brandon, I would gather mothers who lost children, women like Shirley Thomas or my friend Tamika Felder, and put them all up in a hotel. Then I'd schedule them massages or take them on a boat ride. I'd walk the aisles with them at those funerals. But I didn't know that I was planting seeds all along. So many of those same women checked on me when Brandon died. Tamika took one look at me, and her eyes said, *My brother, I know. I remember, and I'm here.*

No matter what problems me or my children might have had, you could not have made me believe that this is what we'd end up going through.

But then Pastor Bryant said something that completely wiped me out. He said that when he went through the early months after his daughter's death, he had a revelation. "The way I felt, I could've easily found another God to serve if that was possible," he said. "But I told God I didn't know one better than Him."

In true Baptist, praise break fashion, I quickly got up out of my seat and ran to the other side of the church. Then I lay on the floor, between two pews, for about forty minutes with a box of tissue in my hands, crying. That word just hit me in the chest. Because yes, this all hurts. *And* God is real. Yes, this is painful. *But* I was not going to let it take me out. The truth is, if I had never seen or felt God a day in my life, I certainly did after Brandon passed. Had I not, I'm fairly certain I'd be dead. God has kept me. Kept me alive and given me the strength to keep going.

All right, God. I'm going to show You. Going to let my son come home to You? Well, I'm going to show You that I'm still going to serve You.

Perhaps the most profound moment of gratitude came from the most unexpected place. As I've shared, the Wednesday after Brandon passed, I went to work and then afterward I went home to gather Brandon's funeral clothes, which I threw in the back of my Jeep. Before heading to the funeral home, I stopped by the Salvation

Army, put on an apron, and went to feed the homeless. While this is something I do often, on that day, it was something I needed to do. Why? I guess I needed to see my privilege in all this. In that cafeteria, there were people who'd stood in line forever for a hot dog with sauerkraut, a handful of chips, something to drink, and a slice of cake. People who held so much gratitude in their eyes as I handed them their meal. They knew despair for sure. And yet they still said, "Hey, Rick, I heard what happened. I'm so sorry for your loss," or, "Yeah, man. My son got killed not too long ago. Praying for you."

Going to serve at the Salvation Army was a way for me to get some gratitude in my soul. Sometimes that thankfulness isn't going to just land on you. The pain is too deep. You have to step outside of yourself and find gratitude. And then when you get it, you hold on to it for dear life. When I walked out of the Salvation Army that day, it was dark, cloudy, and raining. I still had to go to the funeral home and drop off Brandon's clothes. I couldn't listen to any soft rock like I might have done on an ordinary day because Brandon loved all that. Couldn't listen to the Groove 30 channel because Brandon loved that too. So I just held on to the gratitude that had just been given to me. I told myself, "I get to serve my son in this way. I get to get his clothes together." Even in my grief, I needed to be humbled. I needed to see my world—though forever changed—not just through the lens of my own pain. Helping people whose journeys were infinitely harder than mine was a stark reminder of how blessed I still was.

Since then, I've continued to try to find ways to give back. Maybe even especially when the shadow of darkness returns and my heart breaks all over again as it does now regularly. Sometimes that looks

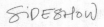

like serving food to the homeless. Other times that's responding to the emails and direct messages of people all around the country who listen to me on the radio or have seen me at a show and have experienced similar losses. Often they don't know what to do or how to go on, and just a kind word from me helps right them when they think they are going to fall or jump off the cliff of their pain.

One of the first things I tell people who are grieving is to find a way to get out and do something for somebody else. Go serve somebody else. Sometimes that alone will steady you when you are getting smacked around by the pain. Even though many therapists might not initially recommend service as a way to heal because they believe it's important to take care of yourself first in those moments, I find that helping other people is the best way to take care of myself. It gives me much-needed perspective.

Connecting to the suffering of others helps me not make everything about me and my pain. It helps me realize that people are losing children every day. My adopted niece, Melva, lives in Birmingham. My grandmother and her grandmother lived next door to each other. She's much younger than me, so she has always called me Uncle Rickey because I grew up with her uncles.

Well, her nineteen-year-old daughter was killed a year ago, and she has been going through it. Because of this, I will sometimes buy her a plane ticket and hotel room to see one of my shows so she can just hang out. Rest her heart a little bit. That's what *I* can do. But you might be able to do something else. Maybe you can start a meal train for a family who has lost a loved one. Give a friend a ride who isn't up to driving themselves to the hospital to see their baby hooked up to machines. Maybe you just sit quietly on a park bench with an elder who is trying their best to hold on to memories.

When you can step outside of yourself and start caring for other people in the midst of your pain, I believe God extends you a little grace that lightens your own load. Service, like gratitude, helps lift some of those burdens off us. It's like God gives us just a little bit more space, a little bit more room in our cups.

Acts of service and expressions of gratitude are just as much healing agents as Miss Jannie's words were that day in her house. It takes courage to have gratitude when you've lost someone you love. It takes courage to be present when you are in pain. Gratitude isn't just a coping mechanism. It's a lifeline. It can anchor you when those waves inevitably hit.

Most of us understand that being grateful for what we have is a good thing, and we tend to think we are grateful for the life we live, whether it's been good or bad. We nod in agreement when reminded of the importance of counting our blessings, regardless of the circumstances we find ourselves in. But in our darkest moments, it's easy to overlook the simple act of being thankful. When we decide to be grateful, we uncover gratitude's remarkable ability to heal not just our minds but our bodies and spirits as well. God uses our gratitude to spur us on toward healing.

Consider a garden. We may tend to our plants, watering them

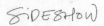

and ensuring they receive adequate sunlight. But do we truly appreciate the intricate dance of life unfolding before us—the relationships between soil, roots, and stems? Gratitude, much like a gardener's tender care, nurtures the seeds of contentment and acceptance within us, allowing them to take root and blossom despite what we've gone through.

I'm thankful for the thirty-two years I had with Brandon on this side of glory. I thank God for those thirty-two years because I know there's a mother out there who got only five years, a father out there who got only sixteen years. When I can truly say I'm grateful, something else happens. A level of acceptance comes over me. And when I embrace that acceptance, I can face the really hard thing. The knowledge that I won't get a thirty-third year with Brandon. See, acceptance doesn't mean being complacent; rather, it is a recognition of what is and what cannot be changed. That degree of acceptance usually leads to a kind of contentment. It leads me to a place where I don't try to manufacture something different for my life, some different reality. I live with the fact that I have been preceded in death by my child. Then I turn that contentment into a calm that allows me to get a better grasp on my emotions when they show up.

To me, the opposite of gratitude is entitlement. It blinds us to the truth. Entitlement lies to us, making us believe we are somehow exempt from trials and tribulations. It's the belief that no bad thing should happen to me or my family members. But who am I to say that? I mean, of course I don't want bad things to happen. No one does. But in the big scheme of this world, who am I to demand to not experience the pain of loss? Who am I to feel as though I'm entitled to never have to grieve?

There are certainly big, grand reasons to be grateful. I'm thankful to have three other beautiful children who are still pressing on and still here with me. But there's also the little things. The small moments of gratitude. Sometimes when grief has taken over to the extent that anxiety and depression have settled into your body, the only gratitude you might be able to muster is, "Thank You, God, for allowing me to get out of bed today." Or "Thank You, God, for the ability to stay in bed today." Or "Thank You, God, for being able to take a shower or eat a bowl of Froot Loops or take a walk or for the phone call from my aunt." These simple, small moments of gratitude add up. They shift your lens. They make you think about what you have as opposed to what you don't have, what's here and present as opposed to what's not here and gone. And that's such a big deal on this healing journey.

There will absolutely be moments when you don't want to be grateful. When you'll want to scream to anyone who'll listen that you'll never accept this loss. But whether you accept it or not, what is . . . is. And getting to acceptance is only for your benefit. It's not changing what happened. It's not saying what happened is okay. It's just helping you get to a point where, first, you can function and survive, and second, maybe eventually thrive.

14

DETERMINED TO
LAUGH AND HEAL

*Please never forget how brave it is to continue
to show up in a story that looks so different
than what you'd thought it'd be.*
—Liz Newman

IT WAS A HOT SUMMER DAY AT HARTSFIELD-JACKSON
Atlanta International Airport, a few years before Brandon passed.
My flight was delayed, so I did what so many of us do when we're
killing time—scroll social media. As I swiped the images on my
Facebook news feed, I saw everyone living their best lives. Friends
and followers alike were on vacation. Some were enjoying family
and class reunion celebrations. Others were going to all-white day
parties or brunches in their flyest clothes. There was so much joy in

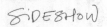

the smiles they flashed in those photos, and so much pure laughter in those videos, that it caused me to reflect on my own life.

What about me?

And I absolutely didn't mean that in an envious way. I know better than anybody that social media is a highlight reel. It's never the whole story. I didn't begrudge anyone their fun, nor was I necessarily wanting what they had. But those images did remind me that I wanted more. More family. More rest. More time to enjoy the fruits of my labor. I hadn't chosen joy for myself in a long time. I finally said, "Enough is enough."

As I sat in the airport, headed for a show in Tulsa, Oklahoma, I was absolutely grateful for the work I get to do. I get to make people laugh, and that's one hell of a calling. I'm thankful that people are always excited to see me perform. But it can also be a monotonous gig. Sitting in that terminal, I realized I was stuck in a cycle of performing and traveling that often meant I spent most nights alone in a hotel room watching TV or, yes, scrolling the internet. Then I went to the next city to do it all over again. Year after year, it's the same thing. It can be a lonely existence.

Something needed to change.

So I made a bold move. I canceled all my commitments for that summer, sold some property, and bought a boat. Then I decided to live on that boat for the rest of the summer. Let me tell you, it was the best decision I ever made.

For six weeks that year, I soaked up the sun in Fort Lauderdale. The marina was right across the street from the beach, and I did nothing but lounge there and live life at my own pace. It was pure bliss. And a revelation. Who knew that I could have more joy, more rest, more overall happiness by simply choosing it for myself? I did it for five years before Brandon passed and I plan to do it every summer after. Maybe I'll do a few shows here and there to keep my edge, but I'm at the point in my life where I refuse to sacrifice my well-being for the sake of work. That knowledge, that practice of self-care, has absolutely been helpful on this grief journey.

And it's not just about taking a break from work. It's not about the boat or the vacation. I know that not everyone can just leave work for six weeks. It always feels good to have a change of scenery, but sometimes it just isn't possible.

But what *can* you do?

You might not be able to take off work for a long period of time, but you can take a twenty-minute nap when you need it. You can take a walk around the block when feeling stressed. People see me constantly moving and think I'm always on the go. But the truth is, I do prioritize rest. The meetings I have—whether they're conference calls with agents, talking to writers, cracking jokes with other comedians—don't require much ripping and running, as the elders used to say. Yes, I've got my shows and the morning show gig, but I also make sure to hit the sack early. I'm talking lights out by 6:30 p.m. since I usually have to be up at 3:00 a.m. I value those nine hours of sleep. I pop my vitamins too. I take 5,000 IUs of vitamin D and omega fish oil, which is an anti-inflammatory. I take a multivitamin, probiotics, and if it has been a particularly busy week, I might even get a nutritional IV to help me remain healthy. I also get regular massages and eat relatively well (although I'm still a Southern cook, so you know I'm going to slip up now and again).

I know many men think self-care is the domain of women.

We've bought the lie given to us by advertisers and even some in the wellness industry. We have a very narrow definition of self-care that calls to mind nail and salon appointments. But it's just as important for men, Black men especially, to make caring for the mind, body, and spirit a priority. I know better than ever that life is too short to neglect that.

Taking care of our bodies is so important, especially when we're grieving, because grief can bring on anxiety in the worst way. My anxiety is real deep. It's that sick, run-to-the-bathroom type of butterflies in the stomach. It's that feeling that Brandon has just died even though it's been a year. The kind of anxiety that doesn't always show up in my tears but just in this sinking feeling on the inside.

But you know what else helps? Laughing. Watching funny videos on Instagram and YouTube. I watch the comedians I love. I go do my morning show and laugh with my team Rock-T, Special K, Maria, Gary, and Brat. Doing that five days a week gives me something to look forward to. I know there will be smiles awaiting me in the studio. I know that we will laugh.

Even when I'm performing, I'm laughing. Because I need that dose of medicine like the audience does. I enjoy watching other people laugh. I get a kick out of high-fiving people as I walk out into the audience. Giving joy gives me joy.

After Brandon died, I was heading to Fort Lauderdale when I met a man who was on his way to rehab. I was wearing a white jacket and some white sneakers and this dude started cracking jokes on it. He was roasting me so bad, and it was so good. I asked him where he was going and he said, "I'm going to rehab."

"What?! Oh, you done messed up now, brother."

With his permission, I went live on Instagram, and we took the roasting to the world. I said, "This man is roasting me but he's going to rehab. How you talkin' about my shoes and your eyes are roasted? This brother's eyes is burgundy, y'all." And we just went back and forth. It was so funny, but more than anything, I think it made both of our days. He likely needed that laugh before doing some of the hardest work of his life—getting off drugs. And I needed the laugh before doing one of the hardest things I've ever had to do in my life—grieve my son who could not get off drugs.

———————

Healing from the loss of a child ain't easy. Y'all get that yet? Your kids are like your limbs. When we wake up every day, before we count our fingers and our toes, we unconsciously count our kids. It's devastating to realize that every morning when you wake up, you must remember that you have a limb missing. When your child is gone, it feels like a piece of you is missing. So yes, healing is a process, but self-care is one part of that process. It has to be a non-negotiable if you want to be well when that grief rears its head.

I know now that I deserve to be taken care of the way that I've taken care of people all my life. I deserve to have people show up for me the way I've shown up for people. I know now that sometimes I have to go inward and tend to my own heart before focusing on what's going on outside of me. This is how I can keep living. How all of us can keep living. This is how I've learned to not allow grief and loneliness to consume me.

It's true what they say about having to embrace a "new normal" once you've lost a child. Things are never the same. I can never go back to the day before Brandon died. I can't change a single thing about anything that occurred during his lifetime. And that's hard to hold at times. It's hard not to think about what might have been. Especially when I look in the face of his daughter. There have been so many days when the pain has been so unbearable that all I can do is cry. In those moments, I'm grateful for the nine hours of sleep I get each night. I'm glad for the summers of rest and relaxation that give me space to feel everything I need to. It's so important to have something in place to help you out of the hole when those moments come. Therapy, self-care, and laughter are a really good start.

Yes, laughter again. Comedy is always going to be where I land in this sideshow called life. I'm determined to keep laughing. More than anything else, that's how I'm healing. That's how I'm helping others heal. Whether it's watching funny videos online or roasting and cracking jokes with friends, laughter can be medicine. It is a constant reminder that there's still light in the darkness. Even if you have to use laughter as a way to crawl into the next day, do it. Because the next day might have a little more light for you.

There are so many ways that laughter heals. Its therapeutic effects extend far beyond just offering passing relief. Laughter can uplift spirits, ease pain, and even make us physically well. I know this as a comedian. I've seen how laughter has transformed a person's mood, even my own. But I also realize that not everyone has the luxury of having a job that forces them to laugh. That doesn't mean you can't have joy. Your joy just might look different. Your joy might actually take a little bit more work to locate and access. You might realize you can't watch reality shows anymore because that's something you used to watch and talk about with your loved one. But you might find that you've acquired a new love for romance novels or thrillers. What do you do then? Do you dwell on what you can't do anymore? Do you add to your grief? Or do you decide to do a new thing? To reclaim your joy? Do you say, "I'm going to read that new romance this week," or, "I'm going to the movies to check out that thriller next week"? Whatever it takes to make you smile or laugh, do that.

I know someone who, when she got really sick after grieving the loss of a family member, watched every stand-up comedy special on Netflix. Yes, literally every single one. She turned to stand-up comedy as a source of solace and watched every special from Nigeria to Australia, Germany to America. She watched comedians she'd never heard of and the ones who were her favorites. Famous or obscure, she absorbed them all. The laughter she intentionally incorporated into her life became an anchor, not just for her emotional well-being but also for her physical health. She would tell you that as she laughed her way through each special, she began to notice an improvement in her overall condition. The laughter helped her heal. From that first day forward, she continues to make laughter a huge part of her life. All so she can be and stay well.

There's power in laughter. For real. Studies have shown that the body's physiological response to genuine laughter is remarkably similar to that of fake laughter and might even be able to help lower blood pressure and minimize stress.[1] This must mean that even if you're not feeling particularly happy, engaging in laughter exercises or deliberately seeking out sources of laughter can still yield positive effects. In essence, the body simply responds to the act of laughter itself. Meaning, you could start laughing right now,

just break out for no reason, and your body will translate that as a response to pleasure. So, whether you're genuinely amused or simply going through the motions, your body reaps the same benefits. It will send out all those feel-good hormones regardless. The Mayo Clinic even says that laughter releases endorphins and decreases stress hormones, contributing to enhanced immune function and overall well-being.[2] That's how powerful our laughter is. Plus, I've found that even when people fake laugh, nine times out of ten it turns into an authentic laugh after a while because joy is contagious. We can't help it. If we start laughing for no reason, then we'll end up laughing for all the reasons.

But let's not even try to make it complicated. One of the first things I encourage people to do is to figure out what *they* think is funny. As comedians, it's something we do instinctually. We have an innate sense of what's funny to us, which drives our ability to sit down and write jokes and then stand up and deliver them. It's where the best characters are born. And most of the time, the funniest things come from our everyday lives. Our memories. We have an acute awareness of what's funny, and that's a skill that even folks who are not comedians can absolutely acquire for themselves.

What would it look like to sit down and make a list of all the things you find funny? Or to spend the week just paying attention to all the times you laugh? Did someone at work tell a hilarious joke? Was there a funny scene in a movie? Pay attention to the moments throughout your day when you find yourself smiling or chuckling and take note of what triggered those reactions. By writing these instances down, you'll gain insight into your unique sense of humor and what brings you joy.

Once you've compiled your list of things that either made you laugh in the past or are currently making you laugh, the next step is to integrate them into your daily life. Be intentional about recreating those "funnies" on a daily, weekly, or monthly basis. Treat laughter as part of your self-care routine, just like exercise or prayer. I truly believe this is the kind of medicine we all need. The kind of medicine that will help our bodies become stronger as we deal with those waves of grief. The kind of medicine we can prescribe ourselves.

Listen, I want all the joy I can stand. My grandkids bring me joy. Performing onstage brings me joy. Listening to soft rock, when I can, brings me joy. Driving my boat to Bimini, Bahamas, and swimming with sharks and stingrays brings me joy. I get joy from going to Honeymoon Harbor, dropping an anchor, and diving into the ocean where the water is so blue I can almost see all the way through it.

Cooking for people brings a lot of joy also. Some of my best days are when I put my radio station on XM Groove and get to cooking Italian, Cajun, or soul food in my kitchen. I'm a foodie who likes to prepare food and watch people eat it. I get that from my grandmother. It gives me the same feeling that watching people laugh at my jokes does. In fact, as hard as I work for an audience who has paid to see me, I work just as hard for people who are going to sit down at my table and eat. Both fill me with a much-needed, healing kind of joy.

Grief changes you, for sure. I've said that over and over again here. It leaves scars, both seen and unseen. I will never be the same Rickey Smiley I was before January 29, 2023. But my grief has also taught me resilience. It's taught me that what I do with my pain matters. I've chosen to keep living. To keep laughing. I hope you do too.

EPILOGUE

DOUBLE FOR MY TROUBLE

I will restore to you the years that the
swarming locust has eaten.
—JOEL 2:25

"THEY'RE MINE? I HAVE TWINS? TWO LITTLE GIRLS?"

Sometimes you have to just marvel at the way God works. Just when I thought my heart couldn't hold any more joy or pain, God surprised me with a revelation that turned my world upside down, in the best possible way.

I opened this book sharing the moment when I got the worst news of my life. It's only fitting that I end it with one of the most redeeming pieces of news I've ever received. On the day I discovered that I am the father of two beautiful, four-year-old twin girls, the news hit me like a ton of bricks. So many feelings filled my body. Shock. Happiness. Excitement. And complete and utter joy. And the kicker? I found out about them within days of the first anniversary of Brandon's passing. How could I have known that day when I could barely walk down the hallway after getting the call about Brandon that I would, almost exactly a year later, walk into a house filled with giggles and love and a double dose of Black girl magic? As I said earlier in this book: God, like He did with Job, sometimes gives us "double for our trouble." But now that's not an abstract, way-out-there notion. It's about as real as real can get. And for me, quite literal.

The first night the twins spent the night with me as their dad was the night before the fifth birthday celebration I'd helped put together with their mother. I also had my other grandson over. Watching them play and laugh brought on a bittersweet feeling. There was the ever-present pain of loss. The memories of when Brandon was their age. But then there was the presence of new, boundless love.

Our time together was a blast. I got up at 4 a.m. with them to watch *Peppa Pig*, apparently one of their favorite shows. I even bunked in their room, determined not to let them wake up in the dark feeling alone in a house they weren't as familiar with. I went from trundle bed to trundle bed, helping them get to sleep. Every time one would wake up, I'd go over to that one's bed and pull the bottom out.

As I navigated the day, teaching them manners ("No, it's not, 'I want some cereal,' it's, 'May I have some cereal?'") and redirecting all their energetic shenanigans, I couldn't help but feel a sense of healing wash over me. These girls, my daughters, were a new chapter in my journey of fatherhood—one that, at fifty-five years old, I hadn't expected. Even though it was heavy knowing Brandon would never get the chance to meet them, they are still a blessing that I wanted and needed to hold tight.

God, in His grace and mercy, has kept His promise to me. To restore the years. To be with me through my pain and redeem it somehow. To turn everything for my good. Some might call it coincidence. Others might get hung up on my not being married or want to know more about the dynamics of the previous relationship that gave birth to the girls. But honestly, that's not the story here. Their mother was a woman with whom I'm very good friends but who I also had an off-again, on-again relationship with several years ago. That's it. The greater story here is how, even in the midst of great grief, God has intervened. It's about how God can take pain, shortcomings, and flaws and transform them into something that still gives Him glory and still works out for our good. Remember that? Well, that's how I see my two new babies. As a demonstration of God's love, grace, and redemption. He had a plan all along. A plan to heal my broken heart and fill it with the light of new beginnings.

And you know what's so absolutely extraordinary (but totally God) about this new development in my life? The whole month prior to learning about their paternity, everything was terrible. January was already going to be a hard month for me. It was hard not to dread the anniversary of Brandon's death. But I got no breaks. No chance to even breathe.

The year 2024 started out relentless. First, on January 4, there was the uproar stirred by Katt Williams's words in an interview on Shannon Sharpe's YouTube podcast, *Club Shay Shay*. All hell broke loose when that interview hit the internet. In the interview Katt said, "He [me] told everybody, 'It should have been my role!'

[Money Mike in *Friday After Next*]" and "He was so egregious that I put in my contract that I wouldn't work with Rickey Smiley again unless he's in a dress."[1] Whew! What a hit. I truly felt like I was being painted as the villain of the hour. I mean, I was minding my own business, doing my radio thing, when suddenly, according to how I was interpreting the comments I was seeing on the internet, I was the bad guy, the hated one. It felt like I had been thrown into the lion's den, and everyone was ready to tear me apart. So much so that I found myself buried under a barrage of what I thought was slander and scrutiny.

Everyone had an opinion. It didn't matter that I went live on-air and tried to offer some clarity. It didn't matter that I tried to show as much grace as possible because, honestly, all I could think about was the looming date of January 29 and the one-year anniversary of Brandon's death. The blogs and their rumors didn't care about none of that because, to me, they thrive on chaos. Nevertheless, I was so taken off guard when my name was mentioned. *Where is all this vitriol toward me coming from?*

The thing is, what Katt said about me wasn't what I was mostly concerned about. It certainly didn't make things better, especially given the response it received. I was more worried about January 29 and how it was affecting my mental health. How it might affect my children. I was in Florida getting therapy twice a week and looking at the ocean every day. I was going to physical therapy every other day because I'd begun to have some upper-back spasms. Here I was, trying to just be well, and it felt like the world was exploding around me.

Then, to pile on, I'd heard from some of my brothers of Omega

Psi Phi Fraternity, Inc., that other brothers were turning on me because in a moment that was already filled with anxiety, I'd stumbled and mentioned only three of our organization's four cardinal principles. The comment sections of posts were filled with frat brothers who showed no grace. Never mind that my head was spinning. That my brain misfired and didn't push out the word *perseverance* because I was trying to address the whole Katt Williams thing and I had my producer in my ear yelling, "Go to commercial, go to commercial!" I didn't get it out and the bruhs lost it.

I love my brothers. Most people know that. And I know how important our principles of Manhood, Scholarship, Perseverance, and Uplift are because I do my absolute best to live that out every day. Omega Psi Phi is more than just a fraternity to me. My bruhs are family. I've been through thick and thin with many of them. So when some of them turned their backs on me, it hurt. When I heard that quite a few had jumped on the "Rickey Smiley ain't nothing" bandwagon, even to the extent of making T-shirts about me, I couldn't help but feel betrayed.

After all the drama of January 2024 hit, I did what I knew to do. What my grandparents and great-grandparents had taught me to do. I got on my knees and prayed. I said, "God, I need a win. Please."

And He answered me.

God said, *Don't worry, Rickey. Do not be afraid. You're not going to go through that again. You're not going to feel that way again. I got something for you because you have been dedicated. You have been committed. You did not stray away from Me. You did My will.*

195

I was completely surrendered during and after that prayer. I didn't care anymore about my career, despite loving what I do. The entertainment business is hard and tainted in a lot of ways, so I don't really want to be any more famous than I am already. I don't need no more TV shows or movies, especially if they come with all the unconstructive criticism from armchair philosophers hiding behind an avatar on the internet. I needed some other kind of win.

"What can You possibly do for me, God?" I asked. And I wasn't talking about money either. Not comedy tours. None of that.

Then God, I imagine, was like, *Bet. I got you.*

And you know what? God did what He said. He didn't let any of that mess break me. I had to remind myself that I had nothing to hide and nothing to be ashamed of. Especially when it came to my career and all the rumors and headlines like "Rickey Smiley's Career Is Over."

I felt emasculated in front of the entire country all because I played a character who happens to be a woman and who actually started on the radio like many characters do. I know who I am as a man. I'm a confident Black man raised by Ernest Smiley. So I don't care what people think about me doing the Bernice Jenkins character. If they want to sexualize it or equate it to cross-dressing, then so be it. As long as they remember that Bernice is a character people laughed at heartily and enjoyed before it became taboo to do so. And my job is to make people laugh, period.

If I'm honest, it all felt like God was toughening me up. Maybe so the twenty-ninth would be easier to endure? I truly believe God used all that drama for my good. As the days passed and the noise died down, I found safety in the love and support of my family, friends, and fans who have rocked me since forever. I also realized something pretty profound about everything that happened leading up to the anniversary of Brandon's death. God didn't *cause* the drama I was experiencing—that responsibility lies squarely with the people in the mix. But God, once again, did use the chaos and turmoil to strengthen me. To remind me of what truly matters. It felt like a protective measure. A way to get me to January 29 with the clear understanding that I can and have survived many things. And when that day finally did roll around and the weight of grief threatened to crush me, I stood tall and chose joy to celebrate the life of my boy.

On the first anniversary, I brought my whole family to Florida for a boat ride. And when I tell you we had a good time?! We had good music and good food. We celebrated that weekend the way I know Brandon would have wanted. I didn't get to decide what happened January 29, 2023, but I did get to decide what happened January 29, 2024, and I decided to choose life. To choose love. To choose laughter and joy.

As I stood in the doorway and watched my two little girls play in a room of my home that hadn't seen much playtime in years since my other children are grown, I noticed that the heaviness was gone. Their innocence had moved me to tears and a weight was finally lifted. I'd awakened that morning and, for the first time, the sun had its color back. *Hallelujah!*

I still can't tell them apart. I have to ask them their names.

"What's your name?" I asked one.

"I'm Alyssa," she said.

"What's your name?" I asked the other one.

"I'm Allison, Daddy," she said with a little sauce.

Daddy.

Whew. Let me get this right, God.

To wake up with two little girls looking me in my face and telling me they are bored despite me having bought up the toy store in anticipation of their arrival felt like everything was right in the world. For the first time since Brandon's passing, I felt a sense of peace wash over me—a peace that surpasses all understanding. Can I say it again? God has an amazing way of turning our darkest moments into blessings, of bringing light into the darkest of places. Alyssa and Allison are beautiful reminders that even in the darkest of times, there is always hope. They are evidence that I am a man redeemed, surrounded by the imperfect but boundless love of my family. God's plan is greater than anything I could imagine.

Let me be clear. This healing journey was never about me. Not in the sense that God just decided to randomly "gift" me with the knowledge of more children as some kind of reward for my pain. No, no, absolutely not. He's not some cosmic genie that way. This was more about how God used my trials and tragedy to teach me how to trust in His timing. When it felt like all hope was lost and the world around me seemed to crumble, God stepped in and said, *Surrender it all to Me, give Me all that pain, and watch what happens.* I answered Him that day when I was serving at the Salvation Army with the clothes of my dead son in the car. I told God, "I'm trusting You. I'm still going to serve despite everything I'm going through." I totally leaned on God. I didn't curse Him. I felt like I had no choice but to simply obey His will for my life, even when that will hurt.

Now, almost exactly one year later, I get to play with my two baby girls. That feels like more abundance than I can hold.

I can talk about how good God is longer than anybody else. Because I believe it. And I know that for some people, that's hard. They see all the terrible things happening in the world, the state of our country, the state of their own lives, and they can't see anything else. Especially not the goodness of an all-knowing, all-seeing God. I get it. And to them I say, "What's the alternative?"

Imagine me having two windows in front of me. Through one window, I see my son is dead. Because of that I'm depressed. I'm broken. This is a real window with real things I'm seeing happening in my life. But then there's another window. In window number two, I see that my son is not suffering anymore. I see that I'm still sad but I'm able to go get some help via therapy. I can believe God has something better down the road for me if I trust Him like I've never trusted before. Which window is going to give me a better quality of life? Which perspective is going to help me heal and have more joy even in the midst of my pain?

So I did what I had to do. I chose a different way of seeing what happened. I remembered what my grandparents taught me. What the Mississippi Mass Choir sang: "I know the Lord will take care of me. I know the Lord will provide for me."[2]

Gospel artist Kurt Carr has a song that is so hard for me to listen to sometimes because it will send me to another place. "For Every Mountain" reminds me of just how much I've gone through in my life but also just how much God has been there with me every step of the way:

"For every blessing, Hallelujah, for this I give You praise."[3]

So as I embark on this new chapter of my life—as a father to two more baby girls—I can't help but feel a sense of gratitude. Gratitude for the blessings that have come my way, and gratitude for the lessons learned along the way. For every mountain I've climbed, for every trial I've faced, I give thanks. And as I look ahead to the future, I do so with hope in my heart and a song of praise on my lips. Life might feel like a circus sideshow, but I also know that no matter what lies ahead, God is always there by my side.

ACKNOWLEDGMENTS

FIRST, I'M GIVING HONOR TO GOD WHO IS THE HEAD OF my life . . . (Now, y'all know that's how churchy Black folks love to open every speech.)

There are so many people I want to thank for making the telling of my story, this book, possible.

To my mother and father, Carolita and Edward Lester, I'm so grateful for the lessons you both have given me. Without you, there is no me.

To my children, Malik Smiley, D'essence Smiley, Aaryn Smiley, Allison, and Alyssa: I love you more than I can even say. Thank you for accepting both the good and not-so-great parts of me as your dad. Thank you for loving me no matter what.

To all those who have stood in the gap for me, in some way, during this season of grief—Pastor Kelvin Bryant and Faith Walkers Church; Pastor Michael K. Moore and Faith Chapel Christian Center; Rachel Arrington Funeral Home; Pastor Walter Solomon; Pastor John King; Bishop Joseph Walker; Le'Andria Johnson; Darlene McCoy; Dr. Bobbie Knight and the Miles College staff; President Joe Biden; Vice President Kamala Harris; the Alpha Phi Chapter of Omega Psi Phi Fraternity, Inc.; Mrs. Thandi Wells; Pastor Keith Norman; Smokie Norful; Brian Stutson; Ms. Jannie;

and so many more. If your name is not here, please, please charge it to my head and not my heart: know that I love you and am thankful for your prayers and support.

To my team at Radio One and Reach Media Management; my business manager, Laura Lizer; Levity Talent Management; Caprenia Anthony; and Sheila Reedus: your support is something I could never take for granted. Thank you, thank you, thank you.

To my *Rickey Smiley Morning Show* team and staff, including Special K, Da Brat, Gary With Da Tea, Headkrack, Rock-T, and Jeff Johnson: y'all held me down during the darkest season of my life. I will never forget that. Love all of you.

To my friends and comrades in comedy—Steve Harvey, Martin Lawrence, Benji Brown, DeRay Davis, Chico Bean, Pretty Vee, B. Simone, Marvin Hunter, Sean Larkins, Rita Brent—thank you for keeping me laughing and for checking on me when I needed it most.

To Latoya, Chuck, Willie, Rachel, Kisa: I cannot thank you enough for all you've done for me.

To the entire team at W Publishing/HarperCollins, including my editor, Carrie Marrs: I'm so grateful for all the ways you have supported and been a champion of me and this book.

To everyone at Creative Artists Agency, especially Cait Hoyt-Walden: thank you for finding the best home for my story. I appreciate you so much.

To Tracey Michae'l Lewis-Giggetts, thank you for everything you've done to help me get this story out of me and onto the page. We did that! I'm so grateful.

And to every single person, near or far, who has sincerely prayed for me and my family: thank you so much. God heard you.

NOTES

Introduction

1. "God Is Good," Jonathan McReynolds, *Make More Room*, MNRK Music Group, 2018.
2. William Ernest Henley, "Invictus," 1875, Academy of American Poets, https://poets.org/poem/invictus.
3. "Sideshow," track 1 on Blue Magic, *Blue Magic*, Atco, 1974.
4. "The Tears of a Clown," track on Smokey Robinson and the Miracles, *Make It Happen*, Tamla Records, 1967.

Chapter 1

1. "Say It Loud–I'm Black and I'm Proud," track 7 on James Brown, *A Soulful Christmas*, King Records, 1968.

Chapter 2

1. "For the Love of Money," track 6 on The O'Jays, *Ship Ahoy*, Philadelphia International Records, 1973.
2. "How I Got Over," track 5 on Aretha Franklin, *Amazing Grace*, Atlantic, 1972.

Chapter 3

1. Rice University, "For the Brokenhearted, Grief Can Lead to Death," ScienceDaily, October 22, 2018, www.sciencedaily.com/releases/2018/10/181022153512.htm; Christopher Fagundes et al., "Grief, Depressive Symptoms, and Inflammation in the Spousally Bereaved," *Psychoneuroendocrinology* 100 (February 2019): 190–97, https://doi.org/10.1016/j.psyneuen.2018.10.006.

Chapter 4

1. "Straighten Up and Fly Right," single, The King Cole Trio, Capitol 154, 1944.

Chapter 6

1. National Institutes of Health, "Biology of Addiction: Drugs and Alcohol Can Hijack Your Brain," News in Health, October 2015, https://newsinhealth.nih.gov/2015/10/biology-addiction.

Chapter 9

1. "Free Mind," track 3 on Tems, *For Broken Ears*, extended play, Leading Vibes, 2020.
2. Matt Miller, "*WandaVision* Episode Eight's Quote About Grief Has Become the Show's Defining Moment," *Esquire*, March 3, 2021, https://www.esquire.com/entertainment/tv/a35713623/wandavision-episode-8-grief-quote-explained/.

Chapter 10

1. "Neuroscientists Show How Brain Stores Memories of Specific Fears," NYU Center for Neural Science, April 2, 2010, https://www.nyu.edu/about/news-publications/news/2010/april/neuroscientists_show.html.

Chapter 11

1. "Encourage Yourself," track 2 on Donald Lawrence and The Tri-City Singers, *Finalé: Act II*, EMI Gospel, 2006.

Chapter 14

1. Dexter Louie, Karolina Brook, and Elizabeth Frates, "The Laughter Prescription," *American Journal of Lifestyle Medicine* 10, no. 4 (July–August 2016): 262–67, https://www.ncbi.nlm.nih.gov/pmc/articles/PMC6125057/.
2. Mayo Clinic Staff, "Stress Relief from Laughter? It's No Joke,"

Mayo Clinic, September 22, 2023, https://www.mayoclinic.
org/healthy-lifestyle/stress-management/in-depth/stress-relief/
art-20044456.

Epilogue

1. "Katt Williams on Rickey Smiley," Shannon Sharpe, Club Shay
Shay, YouTube, January 3, 2024, https://www.youtube.com/
watch?v=7AHuu3ZkZks.
2. "When I Rose This Morning," track 7 on The Mississippi Mass
Choir, *I'll See You in the Rapture*, Malaco Records, 1996.
3. "For Every Mountain," track 3 on Kurt Carr and The Kurt Carr
Singers, *No One Else*, GospoCentric Records, 1997.

ABOUT THE AUTHOR

RICKEY SMILEY IS A LEGENDARY COMEDIAN, ACTOR, author, television host, and award-winning radio host of the top-rated, nationally syndicated show *The Rickey Smiley Morning Show*, for which he won the Marconi Award (radio equivalent of an Oscar) for Network/Syndicated Person of the Year in both 2017 and 2021.

A comedian for more than thirty years, the Alabama native is constantly performing across the country on his own theater tour and makes special appearances on the REAL TALK Comedy Tour as well as the Martin Lawrence–hosted LIT AF Tour. Rickey's tours often include a live band, which Rickey accompanies as an accomplished pianist and organist. Some of Rickey's fan-favorite characters include Mrs. Bernice Jenkins, Lil' Daryl, Joe Willie, and Beauford. Rickey starred in the stand-up specials *Rickey Smiley: Open Casket Sharp* and *Comedy Central Presents: Rickey Smiley* and has released eight bestselling albums, including the #1 comedy album *Rickey Smiley: Prank Calls 6*. On the big screen, Rickey has been featured in urban classics including *All About the Benjamins*, *Friday After Next*, and *Baggage Claim*.